Beyond the
Age of Innocence

Rebuilding Trust Between America and the World

Kishore Mahbubani

PublicAffairs
New York

To

Anne

Book design by Jane Raese
Text set in Bulmer

Library of Congress Cataloging-in-Publication Data
Mahbubani, Kishore.
Beyond the age of innocence : rebuilding trust between America and the world /
Kishore Mahbubani.
p. cm.
Includes bibliographical references and index.
HC: ISBN-13 978-1-58648-268-8; ISBN 1-58648-268-8
1. United States—Foreign public opinion. 2. United States—Relations—
Foreign countries. 3. Anti-Americanism. I. Title.
E895.M34 2005
327.73'009'0511—dc22
2004043182

2 4 6 8 10 9 7 5 3 1

PBK: ISBN-13 978-1-58648-379-1; ISBN 1-58648-379-X

Contents

Acknowledgments

On 31 May 2002, at the close of the last day of Singapore's presidency of the U.N. Security Council in New York, I was obliged (as Singapore's ambassador to the United Nations then) to host a reception to mark the occasion. But when the last meeting ended that day, I asked my deputy to host the reception on my behalf. I had to rush to the airport to fly back to Singapore, as I had learnt that my father was slipping away. When I arrived back in Singapore and went to the hospital, he was alive but gasping heavily for breath. I sat beside his bed, holding his hand to give him comfort and to signal to him I was there, as he was already beyond speaking. I also asked myself what my thoughts would be if and when I were in his position. In the midst of the sadness I felt as I watched my father fading, one thought that sprang into my mind was whether I had completed writing down all that I wanted to before leaving this earth. My father passed away peacefully a few hours later. But in the few hours I spent by his bedside, I made a vow to finish writing all the books I had been planning to write for several years. This book,

I hope, will be the first of a series that was inspired by my soul-searching at the time of my father's death.

By reminding me that we cannot amend what we have written after we leave the earth, my father's death also made me acutely aware that I should write down what I really want to say, not the things that would please contemporary audiences. I have tried to adhere to the discipline of honesty in the writing of this book.

No learning can be done alone. Much of this book is a result of conversations and meetings I have had all over the world. I would not know where to begin if I were to thank all those who have taught me. But I hope that my friends will recall some of the conversations we have had as they read the book. I have been blessed with close American friends from whom I have learnt so much about the good American society. Similarly, without all the international exposure that I have had, the book could not have been written.

I would like to thank Wendy and Bill Luers and William Shawcross for introducing me to my literary agent, Mort Janklow. Mort, in turn, inspired this book in our very first conversation and introduced me to PublicAffairs, to whom I sent my book proposal. I would like to thank my publishers, especially Peter Osnos and Clive Priddle (who is an editor par excellence), for the faith they have shown in me and the support they have given me. Every book requires research. I have been blessed with two good research assistants, Meredith Angelson and Richard Maass. My three personal assistants during the period when I wrote the book were Kim Jong Lung, Ashokumar Nair, and Jileen Tan. They provided me invaluable assistance. The final writing and editing of the book was done in a one-week stay at the legendary Singapore Raffles Hotel, well known for having hosted many writers.

A few friends of mine kindly agreed to be the "readers" after the manuscript was written. They were Steve Burns, Francis Chong, Khong Yuen Foong, Ann-Petley Jones, and Brian Soucek. My manuscript profited from their comments. Umej Singh Bhatia helped me with the chapter on America and Islam. I am also indebted to Les Gelb, Sam Huntington, Paul Kennedy, Strobe Talbot, Paul Volcker, and Fareed Zakaria for responding so promptly and positively to my request for "blurbs." Their endorsements mean a lot to me.

I also need to emphasize an important point. Much of the learning that infuses the book took place during my thirty-three-year career with the Singapore Foreign Service from 1971 and 2004. I would like to thank all my friends and colleagues in the Singapore Foreign Service for all that they taught me. But I must also emphasize that the views in this book are strictly mine. They do not reflect the views of the Singapore Government. Only I should be held responsible for the views I have expressed here. I have tried to be true to myself, not to the institution that I happily served in for most of my career. This book does not represent the views of a diplomat. It represents, I hope, the views of an individual scholar trying to make sense of the difficult times we live in.

Without my late mother, my family would not have survived our difficult early years. She showed tremendous strength and resolve. I credit her for any steel I may have in my spine. I dedicated my first book, *Can Asians Think?*, to her and I shall always be inspired by her courage and fortitude.

Those who know me well know how much I am indebted to my wife, Anne. I would like to thank her for her patience, her editorial guidance and her wisdom. I could not have written this book without her help and support. I am happy to dedicate this book to her.

Preface

I WROTE THIS BOOK to alert my American friends to a preventable tragedy: the rest of the world turning against America.

The evidence is clear. Both the Pew and Zogby surveys of attitudes toward America have demonstrated how negatively the world views America despite the decades of goodwill that had been allowed to accumulate since World War II. A Pew survey of June 2005 showed that favorable opinions of the United States had fallen sharply even in countries that had traditionally been its friends. From 1999 to 2005, favorable opinions fell from 83 percent to 55 percent in Britain; from 78 percent to 41 percent in Germany; and from 78 percent to 38 percent in Indonesia. A June 2004 Zogby study found that overall opinion of America by Arabs was strongly unfavorable. Reservoirs of goodwill have been steadily replaced with reservoirs of ill-will, even hate, in many parts of the world.

One story illustrates the depth of the problem. In November 2005, I was invited to address the Asian regional meeting of the World Council of Churches in a little town in Sulawesi, an island in Indonesia that has experienced tragic Christian-Muslim conflict.

When I spoke, I put across the arguments in this book, pointing out both the good and the harm America had done. The audience's reaction to my remarks was almost unanimously negative. They all felt that I was not critical *enough* of America. It took me a while to realize that I was addressing a room full of Christians, not Muslims. If America cannot win over the hearts and minds of Christians living outside America, it will have a much harder time with non-Christians, who make up the bulk of the world's population.

Sadly, Americans, too, are turning away from the world. An article by Alkman Granitsas, an Athens-based journalist, made the following observations:

> The truth is that Americans are becoming relatively less—not more—engaged with the world in general. A few facts. Since the early 1970s, the American public has paid less and less attention to foreign affairs. . . . Over the same period, the percentage of American university students studying a foreign language has declined steadily. According to a report funded by the United States Department of Education, in 1965, more than 16 percent of all American university students studied a foreign language. Now only 8.6 percent do so. It has long been known that fewer Americans have passports, and U.S. citizens travel less than their counterparts in other developed economies. . . . And indeed, during the late 1980s and early 1990s, the number of Americans even applying for a passport declined for several years.[1]

The danger that might result from such trends is clear: we may reach a tipping point where global sentiments turn irrevocably against America. The solutions aren't easy. The problem is not

---

[1] Granitsas, Alkman. "Deepening Isolation: Americans tuning out the world." *The Straits Times*, December 1, 2005.

about personalities. It is not about Bush or Clinton. It is about the impact of American power on the world. And the impact is growing. In real terms, we may be experiencing a structural contradiction. The world is shrinking. American power is growing. Hence, almost inevitably, American power wades into and often steps on the lives of people all around the globe. This structural problem needs to be addressed head on.

I believe that a solution is ultimately possible. There was a time not too long ago when American power was perceived to be working in the interests of both America and the world. Americans would not want to live in a world where they are despised. They must listen to one of the wisest aphorisms from their own cultural heritage: Do unto others as you would have them do unto you. A few sacrifices will be needed. But, more importantly, a change in mindset and a change in policies are needed.

Many thoughtful Americans who have read this book have reacted positively to its arguments. I hope that this new paperback edition will bring the argument to an even wider audience—in search of a global consensus when the need for one is greater than ever.

Introduction

> All of the great leaders have had one characteristic in common: it was the willingness to confront unequivocally the major anxiety of their people in their time. This, and not much else, is the essence of leadership.
> — JOHN KENNETH GALBRAITH

I HAVE HAD THE GOOD FORTUNE of enjoying a long and deep engagement with American society. On Thanksgiving Day, 2003, for the sixth year in a row, the family of my wife, Anne (an Irish American born in New Jersey), assembled in our New York apartment. There were thirty-eight of us—family and close friends—including eleven American first cousins of our three children. When I think of the great virtues of American society, I think of these Thanksgiving evenings. And I think what a blessed society America is to have created such a warm and caring community among its citizens. The generosity that individual Americans practice towards each other is rarely matched in other societies.

I have had the equal good fortune of a long and deep engagement with the rest of the world. Perhaps one of the greatest blessings of my life is that I have experienced directly many of the key political and cultural currents that have swept through our world in the past half century. I was born into a poor family in Singapore, then a British colony. I grew up in a Hindu household, living with Islamic families as neighbors on both sides of our home, in the Chinese majority society of Singapore. Growing up in such an environment, I understood the Western dominance that has influenced the course of history in recent centuries. But I also appreciated the souls of the Hindus, Muslims, and the Chinese, who combined make up over half the population of the world. My life circumstances gave me an unusual perch to understand the world, especially a world that is changing so fast.

As I grew up in the era of increasing American global dominance, I also began to experience and understand how much America had affected the world. Without intending to do so, America had entered into the lives of virtually every citizen on this planet. American leaders have spoken of America as a city on the hill. They saw America as a symbol, providing inspiration even from a distance. Instead, as a result of the technological forces that America had unleashed, distance literally disappeared. America began to enter the lives of all citizens directly.

Tom Friedman of the *New York Times*, who has probably done more than any other American columnist to explain the changing world to Americans, once tried to write "A Theory of Everything" in 800 words. In it he stated that "U.S. power, culture and economic ideas about how society should be organized became so dominant (a dominance magnified through globalization) that America began to touch people's lives around the planet—'more than their own governments,' as a Pakistan diplomat once said to me. Yes, we began to touch people's lives—directly or indirectly—more than their own governments."[1]

America has done more than touch the lives of the six billion occupants of our globe. It has also dominated a global order that each human society has no choice but to adapt to. America decides, the rest of the world adjusts. I have yet to meet an American who wants to dominate the world. This is a great virtue. Unfortunately, it is balanced by the equally sad reality that few Americans understand how much America actually dominates the world. This is one of the key sources of global misunderstanding. America has done more than any other country to change the world. Yet, paradoxically, America is one of the countries least prepared to handle the world it has changed.

The course of the twenty-first century will be determined by the relationship that America develops with the world. The first two centuries of American history should give the world room for optimism. America has almost always been a benign power (except perhaps in Latin America). It has conquered the world with its ideas, values, and management systems (and not, as commonly believed, with its military might). America has been a city on the hill. Its technology has fundamentally changed human history, fueling the most explosive economic growth ever seen. Hence it would only be natural for any American to believe that the prescription for the twenty-first century should be a simple one: Let's have more of the same.

The purpose of this book is to suggest that steady-as-it-goes is not an option. Not for America. Not for the world. The twenty-first century is almost certainly headed for trouble if we sail into it with nineteenth- or even twentieth-century mental maps. We are entering into a new era of human history. We have to consciously discard old mental maps and prepare new ones.

This book is about the next forty years, not the next four years, which provides the time span for the normal political cycle for America. In the course of history, we witness both ripples on the surface and deeper undercurrents. Most times, most politicians in democratic societies focus on the ripples. Their primary goal is to get reelected, not to worry for their electors' grandchildren. Hence there is an almost structural bias against dealing with the deeper undercurrents that will fundamentally change the course of human history.

A simple image may explain the dramatic way in which America has changed the globe. In the past, before globalization brought us together, mankind used to sail in different boats. At points, we connected. But our destinies were shaped primarily by forces inside our boat, not outside. Today, as a result of globalization, we no longer sail on different boats. All our boats have been fused into one. We all sail on the same boat. Let us call it "Spaceship Earth."

This is no abstract analogy. It is an actual description of the state of our world. Increasingly, events that begin in one corner of the globe affect the opposite sides almost immediately. The Asian financial crisis began in Bangkok, Thailand, in July 1997 and eventually reached American shores via Indonesia, Malaysia, South Korea, Russia, and Brazil. The SARS virus began in a village in southern China, reached Hong Kong and from Hong Kong went almost simultaneously to two opposite points of the world, Singapore and Toronto. America escaped SARS by a whisker. But perhaps the best illustration to use for an American audience would be the events of 9/11. A plot hatched in a distant village in Afghanistan led to the demolition of the World Trade Center Towers in New York City. America and Afghanistan are also sailing on the same boat.

There is one fundamental problem with this boat. Each boat needs a captain and crew who take care of the entire boat. Spaceship Earth has none. It does, however, have a dominant power that makes decisions affecting the entire boat. But it makes these decisions not to benefit the entire boat: Its primary interest is in the well-being of the occupants of the dominant cabin, the American cabin. This dominant power does not *intend* to harm the other occupants. But by making decisions that benefit primarily less than 5 percent of the occupants of the ship, resentment develops among the other 95 percent of the occupants of Spaceship Earth. In the same column I mentioned, Tom Friedman quoted Nayan Chanda, the publication director of the Yale Center for the Study of Globalization, as saying, "Where we are now is that you have this sullen anger out in the world at America. Because people realize they are not going to get a vote over American power, they cannot do anything about it, but they will be affected by it."

This sullen anger was not inevitable. Until recently, there were huge reservoirs of goodwill towards America among the six billion other inhabitants of this earth. America had accumulated these reservoirs of goodwill almost absentmindedly, without intending to do so. Indeed, most Americans were probably unaware of these huge reservoirs of goodwill. Tragically, most Americans were also unaware when these reservoirs of goodwill began to be drained away over the past decade or so, to be replaced in some parts of the world, especially in some corners of the Islamic world, by reservoirs of hate and anger. Remarkably, two enormous global processes involving America happened in recent times without Americans taking much notice. This book will try to explain what happened.

Having experienced enough trauma in their history, from the civil war to the civil rights struggle, from the two world wars to the two great wars fought in Asia (Korea and Vietnam), many Americans will resist the idea that they have lived so far in the Age of Innocence. But for all the traumas experienced by Americans, they could still keep two compartments separate in their minds: one for the blessed continent they lived in and the other for the rest of the world. Even those not well-versed in world affairs knew that the rest of the world was a troubled place. America did not have to worry too much over their troubles. They were over there, two oceans away. Americans were over here, living in a comfortable cocoon, physically and psychologically.

The founding fathers of America came to the new world in part to escape the burdens of European history, to avoid getting enmeshed into the long tangled history among European societies. When the Europeans came to America, they gradually dropped their ethnic and national identities and became one. The "melting pot" melted identities and erased history. The rest of the world could get bogged down in history; America had escaped it. This period of innocence is over. America has unleashed forces of globalization that have brought the world to its doorstep. These forces have also increasingly enmeshed America into the tangled webs of history that flow through every other human society. America can no longer stand apart. It must now understand and cope with the history of the world in order to figure out a future for itself. Innocence is no longer an option; ignorance no longer a virtue.

After 9/11, Fareed Zakaria wrote a perceptive and much-talked about cover story for *Newsweek* magazine, "Why Do They Hate Us?" That essay captured the bewilderment of most Americans at being subjected to such a brutal attack. Virtually all Americans felt that they were innocent victims. Most were also probably unaware that in many corners of the world, there were people asking "Why do Americans hate us?'"

The curious paradox here is that America is by far the best educated society on the globe. The percentage of its citizens who have had tertiary education and who have access to all the modern sources of knowledge, from cable TV to the Internet, is among the highest in the world. Yet the American population also appears to be among the least well-informed on global affairs. An American citizen, Mahboob Mahmood (whom I will quote extensively in the chapter on "America and Islam"), made this perceptive observation about the role of foreign policy in the lives of American and Muslim communities:

> I do not know much about foreign policy, but I am well aware of the role of foreign policy in everyday discourse in the Arab world and the rest of the Muslim world. In the United States, foreign affairs are by and large the domain of an intellectual and political elite. In the Arab world (in particular) and the rest of the Muslim world (to a more diluted extent), foreign affairs are part of everyday, bazaar talk. And, in this world, American foreign policy is judged not in terms of the extent to which it advances U.S. interests but the manner in which it affects the recipients and the degree to which it is even-handed.

One hope of this book is to make American society aware that daily, billion of pairs of eyes are watching, studying, and judging America. Their perception is influenced by their geographical location as well as by their history and culture. The movie *Rashomon* made us aware that the same scene can be viewed in different ways through different eyes. This book will provide a few illustrations of how the same global events can be viewed so differently in different corners of the globe.

This may also explain why the language of this book may appear somewhat strange to American critics. American political analysts are accustomed to using a certain range of well-known political concepts to describe contemporary realities. The rest of the world is aware of and also values the deeply held American ideals, but it also is more acutely aware of the gap between high ideals and painful contemporary realities. My hope with this book is to provide American observers a chance to understand that there are also non-American perspectives from which the rest of the world views America and to consider the possibility of alternative descriptions of the contemporary world.

One premise of this book is that many Americans are beginning to be aware that something has gone wrong in America's relations with the world. Many Americans are speaking out about this troubled situation. Anne Marie Slaughter, the dean of the Woodrow Wilson School of Princeton University, wrote an anguished column in the *International Herald Tribune* of May 22, 2004, in which she said, "The world judges us by our deeds rather than our words, and has begun to hold us accountable for our government. This is only fair: we Americans are the preachers and promoters of democracy. If America won't listen, won't consult, won't play by the rules, won't try to see the world through any lenses but its own, can we still be sure that American power is a force for good?"

But I believe that all is not lost. There is hope. There is time. America can turn things around and regain the reservoirs of goodwill that it had both accumulated and lost absentmindedly. To achieve this, it may be helpful to pay more attention to the thoughts and aspirations of the 6.3 billion occupants of our shrinking globe. In so doing, America will only be heeding the wisdom that was the aspiration of its founding fathers: to show "a decent respect to the opinions of mankind."

~ 1 ~

How America Benefits the World

AMERICA HAS DONE MORE GOOD for the rest of the world than any other society. This statement is surely incontestable. The real challenge is to both discover and explain the many ways in which America has helped the world, ways of which most American citizens and officials are unaware.

The single biggest gift that America has shared with the impoverished billions on our planet is hope. America has taught the people of the world that one's fate is not determined at birth. Anyone can succeed in a meritocratic society. America also changed fundamentally the grain of history when it emerged as a major power. It refused to join the European impulse to colonize the world. Instead, America encouraged decolonization. When America was truly powerful at the end of World War II, it sought to create a new world order based on the rule of law and multilateral institutions and processes that also allowed other nations to grow and flourish. No other great power has tried to create a level playing field to enable other nations to also succeed. America did. This explains why many nations flourished in the second half of the twentieth century in this new American world order. America also unselfishly shared its great universities with the best minds of the world. Many of those great minds returned home to create their own national success stories. Yet all these points only provide a partial list of how America has benefited the world.

I can make these statements with great personal conviction, since my own life has been directly affected by many of the beneficial forces America has unleashed. I have also traveled a journey which perhaps few others have. I was born in 1948 in Singapore, then one of the poorer societies of the world. Most of my childhood was spent in a one-bedroom house where six of us lived and paid six dollars a month in rent. I have written most of this book while living in a luxurious six-bedroom apartment in Manhattan, which must rank among the top 1 percent of homes in the world. Hence, I have lived among the poorest of the planet and the richest. I believe that I understand those two worlds and how America has actually impacted the poorest of the planet.

My childhood conditions mirrored those of the poorest. At the age of six when I went to school, I was put into a special feeding program for undernourished children. The poverty of my neighborhood inevitably generated social and ethnic tensions. I have vivid memories of a Malay neighbor returning home with blood splattered over his clothes after having been caught as an innocent bystander in Malay-Chinese riots. No less vivid is the image of young Chinese gangsters battling each other with broken beer bottles ten yards from my doorstep. It is hard to erase memories of blood gushing from open wounds. My father arrived in Singapore at the age of thirteen as an orphan with no formal education or proper adult guidance. In the rough Singapore of the 1930s, he fell into the bad habits of smoking, drinking, and gambling excessively.

My father would slide under the bed when rough debt collectors came to prey on our home. By the time I turned thirteen, my father was in jail.

My early life is not unusual. It contained a pattern of existence that is still experienced by billions around the planet. Having lived among those conditions, I know that what truly kills the poor is not just their poverty. It is their lack of hope that tomorrow would be better than today, or the hope that their children could be better off than they are. For most of mankind through most of history, birth was destiny, especially for the very poor. When Europe began to liberate itself from the Dickensian conditions of the industrial revolution, it was one of the earliest social experiments to bring hope and better living conditions to the poorest. But Europe never captured the world's imagination with its story. America did. It did this because America was probably the first major society to demonstrate that a totally non-feudal order could be built: Almost from the very beginning (apart from the slaves), American society had no class barriers. Instead, with each passing generation there were more and more success stories among the very poor. To make it against great odds was part of the American dream.

This American dream is essentially the magical stardust that America has sprinkled into the eyes of many of the poor around the world. America did not intend to do this. Most Americans believe that this American dream has been confined to American shores. But as the world shrank, and as American TV became ubiquitous, along with Pepsi and 7-UP, McDonald's and Kentucky Fried Chicken, the American way of life became known to billions. The poor were astute enough to see America's greatest strength: that it had a created a social order where even the very poor had an opportunity to advance.

American society has given a new confidence not only to the poor, but to all sorts of nationalities, religions, and other groups as well. America has shown the world that any human can succeed. One of the best contemporary examples of this is Arnold Schwarzenegger's journey from being a "lower-middle-class boy in the bland town of Graz [Austria] to governor of California." His story provides hope to all lower-middle-class boys, not just Austrians. "Mr. Schwarzenegger's victory is seen as a signal to the world: look here, we too are somebody."[1] Similarly, the stories of countless other successful American immigrants carry messages of hope to their nations, messages that are having a great effect on the world population.

This sense that America is the society that provides the most hope to its citizens and immigrants was confirmed by a survey done by the Pew Research Center in 2002. It polled 38,000 people in forty-four countries and asked whether "success in life is pretty much determined by forces outside our control." The largest percentage of any population to disagree with this statement was the American population when 65 percent disagreed, more than double the percentage in old world countries like Italy and Germany, and triple that of India, Turkey, and Pakistan. Professor Alan Brinkley of Columbia University has said: "Americans have always had a stronger belief in the ability of the individual than reality would support. The key is the idea of social mobility, the Horatio Alger vision. There's enough truth to that idea for it to survive, but never as much social mobility as the myth suggests."[2] Often, however, myth is more important than reality. The rest of the world has bought the American myth that the best place in the world for any individual to succeed is America.

I have had the good fortune of traveling to most corners of the globe, including to some of the poorest cities. I have seen people living in miniscule tin shacks among thousands in close proximity. Their living conditions must be terrible. Yet, floating above the sea of tin roofs would be dozens of satellite dishes, each linked to many homes. I have seen this in Asia and in Africa. And when I speak to my guides or my drivers during these visits and ask them what is their greatest aspiration, more often than not the answer would be "I would love to go to America." If I asked why, the answer inevitably would be something along the lines: "If I get to America, I will have a chance to succeed."

I understand this aspiration. In my life, I have lived the meritocratic dream, even though I did not live it in America. Through unusual good fortune, Singapore had remarkably wise leadership upon independence in 1965. These leaders decided that Singapore's only resources were human resources. None should be wasted. Any talent anywhere in society would have an opportunity to grow and flourish. Hence, with financial aid and scholarships, and through a merit-based promotion system, I escaped the clutches of poverty. Indeed none of my ancestors either on my father's side or my mother's side had gone to college. I almost did not. At the age of eighteen, I did what all young Sindhi men did: I became a textile salesman, earning one hundred fifty Singapore dollars (then fifty U.S. dollars) a month. But the government miraculously offered me a president's scholarship paying two hundred fifty dollars. My mother wisely decided that, as two hundred fifty dollars was more than one hundred fifty dollars, I should go to the university. It was a close shave but I made it.

The sad part of this story is how rarely it happens in most parts of the world. Societies that deprive their poor of opportunities to develop their talents only damage themselves. Many of the rich in America understand this. They know that there is an implicit social contract with the poor. The poor in America shall be given every opportunity. And when the rich can help, many of them do. American citizens are by far the most philanthropic individuals in the world.

Now that I have socialized with the richest of the planet (and this is one of the artificial perks of being an ambassador in the world's capital), I have observed how many of the rich elites around the world envy their counterparts in America. The rich in America live and move around freely, with little fear of being kidnapped or harassed. By contrast, most rich elites in the world live in gated communities, under heavy guard. I was in Bogota in 1992 as a guest of a senator. While we were having drinks in his apartment (one of the loveliest I had seen), he pointed to a friend's apartment literally across the street where we would be going for dinner. I said "Good, we can walk across." He said "No way!" We went down the elevator to the locked basement garage, got into a car, locked the doors, drove a hundred feet across the street straight into another locked basement garage and then opened our doors to step out. Bogota may be a bit extreme, but I have seen such gated communities frequently in the Third World. The rich in the Third World envy their counterparts in New York City who stroll down Park Avenue or Fifth Avenue to have dinner. Walking freely on the streets is a freedom that few rich people enjoy in most poor cities.

But when the rich of the world flock to America to spend their money in relative security, they may in fact be functioning as social parasites on the social contract that America's rich has established with America's poor. These wealthy visitors refuse to implement (or are unwilling to see the benefits of) this American social contract in their own countries. As long as America provides them a safe haven, they feel no pressure to replicate a similar social contract in their own societies.

It took a great American philosopher, John Rawls, to describe the real value of this social contract. In his seminal work, *A Theory of Justice* (which I will summarize crudely), he suggested that the most just societies are those that any rational person would pick under the "veil of ignorance" (that is, without knowing whether he would be the richest or poorest member of the society he chose). Under the "veil of ignorance," billions around the world would pick America as their society of choice. They know that even if they landed among the ranks of the very poor, there would be an opportunity for them to thrive. Or if not they, their children would certainly be better off. For most societies, this knowledge of America is not an abstract point. In societies all over the world, people know a compatriot who went to America and succeeded. Vartan Gregorian's story of his move from Armenian roots in Iran to America, captured so well in his autobiography, *The Road to Home: My Life and Times*,[3] is a story that is probably replicated in many a society around the world.

Hence, the "hope" that America has shared with billions on the planet is not an abstract hope. It has made billions believe for the first time in generations that poverty may not be an eternal feature of their lives. Once this hope becomes real, things begin to stir. It is reasonably well known now that China and India are two large societies on the move. The reasons for these new positive trends are complex. But at least one key reason is that both China and India are beginning to realize the value of meritocracy. The Chinese Communist Party, despite its name, bears no relationship to its Soviet counterpart, which used to be run by aging bureaucrats. Today, the Chinese Communist Party is almost as ruthless as Harvard in its search for young talent to fill key positions. The average age of the Chinese leadership is now among the youngest in the world, a remarkable achievement for a society that venerates age and has hitherto equated age with wisdom. In India, the Indian Institutes of Technology (IITs), of which there are seven, have for decades boldly admitted students on pure ability regardless of class or caste. A simple straw poll of most of the successful Indian entrepreneurs in America will show a huge proportion of IIT graduates. Now many of these entrepreneurs are returning home to India to make a difference. I have no doubt that the single biggest reason why mankind will continue to prosper and flourish in the twenty-first century will be because the great American practice of meritocracy will increasingly be shared around the world.

American values have influenced the world not just through the demonstration effect of the success of these values in domestic American society. These values have also influenced America's behavior towards the rest of the world. This is another key reason why America has accumulated a vast reservoir of goodwill in most parts of the world (except perhaps in Latin America) over the past century, as it has been guided often by its own democratic tendency not to conquer or dominate other societies.

My own life would have been quite different if America had chosen to extend, rather than terminate, the European colonial era when America emerged as a major power on the world scene. When I was a young child in the 1950s in the British colony of Singapore, the British Empire certainly appeared to be an eternal feature of our political landscape. My parents took it for granted. Both had migrated to Singapore from India, which had been colonized for a century or more (and, as a result of watching my parents' generation, I realized that the Indian mind remained colonized by the British long after India received its political independence in 1947). As a child, the national anthem I sang was *God Save the Queen* (and I can still sing it). We waved the Union Jack when British leaders arrived. We studied British history as though it were ours. When I was six years old, walking to school with a fellow Indian classmate, Morgan, I asked him where he would like to be when he grew up, he said, "London". "Why London?" I asked. He replied, "Because the streets there are paved with gold." That's how deeply colonized we were. The British Empire seemed to be eternal.

Little did I know that already in the first half of the twentieth century, from the days of Woodrow Wilson, America had seeded the ideas and forces that would lead to the end of the Age of Empire. It is conceivable that European imperial domination of the world could have continued for most of the twentieth century if Europe as a continent had not been exhausted by two world wars. But the American reluctance to join the Europeans in grabbing colonial territories (with the exceptions of the Philippines, Guam, and Puerto Rico) and the psychological pressure America applied on the Europeans to decolonize had a profound impact on world history. It opened new opportunities into the lives of billions, including mine.

There are many great mysteries of history: The huge difference between the European and American waves of history is one of them. When the Europeans broke out of their dark ages, mastered science and technology, launched their industrial revolution, and broke out of the clutches of feudalism with their ideas of liberty and democracy, they were the first to build the greatest societies mankind had seen: providing opportunities to all classes. Yet when they ventured into the rest of the world, they did not share their healthy social values with the societies they colonized. Their goal was to dominate, not to uplift. Democracy at home, empire abroad: Few Europeans saw the contradiction in these two impulses. It helped that they could generate myths that they were on civilizing missions. But their deeds rarely matched their words. Empire was seen as a natural outgrowth of national greatness.

When America burst upon the world in the twentieth century, it could have easily reinforced the European wave of world history by adding a layer of American colonial domination to the European layers. The world would not have been surprised if this had happened. Most Americans had European ancestors. They trace their cultural roots through Europe to the great Greek and Roman civilizations. Americans could have just as easily been seduced by the idea of empire in the Age of Empire. But, fortunately for the world, America was not convinced of the merits of empire. Instead,

America, consciously or unconsciously, peeled off the European layers of world history and in so doing opened the door for billions of non-Europeans to enter the modern world.

Given the enormous contribution America has made towards decolonization and thereby to liberating billions of people, it is puzzling that American chattering classes are now fascinated with the idea of "The Age of the American Empire" as the twenty-first century opens. It is true that some of the writing on this subject has been written by British and Canadian writers. Their argument essentially is that America has become so powerful that it has unwittingly become an empire.

This argument that America is already an empire is deeply flawed. For an empire to exist, you need both rulers and the ruled. The American political system is inherently incapable of running an empire. No empire, not even the relatively benign British Empire, was established without a heavy degree of brutality at the point of colonizing. Most people do not like to be ruled by others. They have to be cowed into submission. The recent painful American experience in Iraq only reinforces this point. With all the military power in the world, America appears incapable of subjugating one medium-sized country in the Middle East because it is incapable of administering the kind of brutal suppression the British applied when they conquered Iraq in 1917. All it takes is for one story of sexual abuse of Iraqi prisoners of war to surface. It becomes front-page news. The American defense secretary and American generals have to spend time defending the behavior of their soldiers and consequently further restrain them. In the good old days of empire, the generals who found innovative ways of subduing the natives by depriving them of their dignity and pride would have been rewarded, not punished. The term "benign empire" is an oxymoron. It will be immensely difficult for America to become a true empire.

More importantly, America may have forever banished the notion of empire because it has changed the whole grain of human history. As a result of the values and principles that Harry Truman and Eleanor Roosevelt embedded into the new international order after World War II, it has become both illegitimate and impossible to create empires today. Illegitimate because current international law does not allow imperial domination. For all their power, neither the Soviet Union nor Vietnam could succeed in their respective efforts to colonize Afghanistan and Cambodia. The Soviet empire crashed for many reasons. One reason was that the people ruled by the Soviet empire no longer wanted to be ruled by it.

To put it simply, the people of the world have changed. They have essentially accepted the American claim that each human being has equal rights and equal dignity. I was born a "British subject" and my family and I happily accepted it then. Today, no people in the world are ready to be "subjects" again, whether it be British or Belgian, Soviet or American. No matter how miserable their condition may be, they still want to be masters of their future. This is why military occupation of any country today is inherently difficult. This applies as much to Israel and Palestine as it does to Syria and Lebanon. It even applies to America and Iraq, even though America is struggling to liberate, rather than subjugate, Iraq.

This inherent American desire to liberate rather than subjugate explains why America has accumulated reservoirs of goodwill even in countries with which it has had painful experiences. Take Japan for example. The Japanese should have ample reason to resent America. They fought and lost a bitter war against America in World War II. Till today, Japan remains the only country in the world to have suffered from nuclear bombs. Hiroshima and Nagasaki were bombed by American planes. All this should have left a deep sense of resentment.

Japan's geopolitical insecurity and its consequent reliance on American power for its own national security may be one reason why Japan remains friendly to America (even though it would be natural for the two largest national economies to see themselves as competitors). But there is a genuine fondness towards Americans among the Japanese. Some of the fondness comes from an awareness of the longer history of Japan-American relations. The Japanese consider themselves lucky that their first major encounter with a Western power was with America, rather than a European power. Consequently, Japan had a happier experience than most other Asian countries.

Not many Americans have heard of Commodore Matthew Perry, but it is no exaggeration to say that he triggered a chain of events that began and will continue to lift billions of Asians out of poverty. Perry appeared off the shore of Japan with a few gunboats in 1853. This was not unusual. European gunboats had been prowling the waters of East Asia for a century or more, guarding the valuable trade enterprises of European merchants. One of these enterprises was the opium trade, which grew into an epidemic for the Chinese people, crippling their society. When the Chinese resisted the opium trade, the British replied with force in the First Opium War (1840–1842). Following a decisive Chinese defeat, several Chinese ports were opened to British trade and Hong Kong became a British colony. No Chinese today would suggest that China should commemorate the arrival of British gunboats off the coast of China.

The Japanese are no less nationalist than the Chinese. But in the year 2003, several Japanese intellectuals suggested that there should be a ceremony to commemorate the 150th anniversary of the arrival of Commodore Matthew Perry and his American warships. The American embassy demurred, fearing a nationalist backlash against America. However, any objective discussion would have shown that the arrival of Commodore Perry brought nothing but beneficial effects for Japan. He was not the first Westerner to arrive on Japanese shores. The Portuguese, Dutch, Spanish, and British had all established trading posts there in the sixteenth and seventeenth centuries, and all except the Dutch had either abandoned them as unprofitable or been expelled by the Japanese. The Dutch continued to trade in Japan for 250 years, but they did not try to open Japan to the world in the way that Perry did. Perry was determined that Japan should open itself up to trade. Japan did. The rest is history.

That history has included some terrible missteps, especially in the first half of the twentieth century. But even these may ultimately have had beneficial effects. The Japanese defeat of Russia in 1905 produced the first crack in the European imperial domination of Asia. Jawaharlal Nehru, who led India to independence in 1947, dated his first realization of the possibility of independence for India from British rule to when he saw an Asian power defeat a European power in 1905 in the Russo-Japanese war. Later, the Japanese foolishly tried to emulate the European imperialists in trying to conquer China and Southeast Asia. But even this phase of violent Japanese imperial expansion had one positive effect. When Southeast Asians saw European soldiers being marched away as prisoners of war by the Japanese in World War II, the myth of European invincibility was destroyed. Undoubtedly, the Japanese were far more brutal as colonizers. Their claims to have "liberated" Asia from European colonial rule were not accepted by most Asians. But the Japanese did destroy all prospects for long-term European recolonization of any kind. The acquired deference to Europe had been eradicated.

In some ways, it was ironic that Japan should have been occupied by a Western power after World War II, when it had done so much to smash the European imperial domination of Asia. Fortunately for Japan, it was occupied by America. No period of foreign occupation can be said to be a happy one. But few Japanese have bitter or resentful memories of General MacArthur's occupation. For all the pain and humiliation they suffered then, the Japanese also remembered that General MacArthur took pains to set Japan on the right course. And Japan has known nothing but peace and prosperity since then. Commodore Perry and General MacArthur are therefore the two markers of the long Japanese encounter with America. In both cases, the Japanese believed that they benefited. Hence, the reservoir of goodwill towards America.

Let me mention in passing that the Japanese-American period of engagement was also marked by many individual encounters, many of which set the tone for Japanese perception of Americans. One significant encounter took place very early in the relationship.

America has been transferring the "yeast" for East Asia's recovery for over a century and it was the Japanese who were the first beneficiaries. After the Meiji restoration triggered by Commodore Perry's visit, many Japanese began to go overseas to learn from the best practices of the rest of the world. One of the leading early Japanese reformers was Yukichi Fukuzawa. In his autobiography, he told the story of a harrowing voyage he undertook in a Japanese sailing vessel across the Pacific in which he encountered severe storms. The voyage was lengthened. Fresh water supplies began to run out. On this Japanese vessel were a few American sailors who were being returned to America after their boat had capsized near Japan. Some of the junior American sailors refused to accept the restrictions imposed on fresh water use. They took regular baths. The Japanese captain complained to their American captain, Smith, who was also on the same boat. Smith said in a matter-of-fact manner that the Japanese could shoot any American soldier who violated the fresh water restrictions. Most Americans would see nothing truly remarkable in this story. If there were rules, they should be applied equally to all. No human being should enjoy a special advantage by virtue of his birth or the color of his skin.

Yet, it is unlikely that any European power then would have behaved as generously as America instinctively did.

On Hitsujigaoka Observation Hill overlooking Sapporo City, Japan, there is a statue of an American: Dr. William S. Clark, revered as one of Sapporo's great forefathers and the founder of Hokkaido University. This statue inspires young Japanese every day with Clark's famous words engraved on his pedestal: "Boys, be ambitious." In a way more direct than most, Clark brought American ideology to Japan, encouraging them to grow and prosper.

The Japanese therefore know in their heart of hearts, whatever they may say publicly, that overall, the long process of engagement between Japan and America has resulted in Japanese society benefiting. Some Americans are aware that they have made positive contributions towards Japan. However, fewer are aware that America may have made an equally important contribution to the development of China.

Japan was perhaps the first nation in East Asia to appreciate the virtues of America. One of the latest to appreciate these virtues is probably China. China is one of the oldest continuous nations on earth. Chinese civilization has perhaps the richest heritage of any society. For much of human history Chinese society was at least the equal of, if not ahead of, most human societies. But China has wasted many recent centuries in trying to catch up with the West. The twentieth century has been one of the most traumatic in its long national history. Although Mao Zedong made an enormous contribution by reunifying the country and safeguarding China's independence, it was still true that at the end of his rule, after eight decades of the twentieth century China remained one of the poorest countries on earth.

To China's good fortune, a great leader emerged to take over the helm after the traumatic years of the Cultural Revolution, Deng Xiaoping. History will eventually recognize him as one of the world's greatest leaders, delivering greater improvement to more lives than virtually any other leader. If nineteenth century British utilitarian philosophers had been alive in Deng's time, they would have said that the concrete benefits that he brought to the lives of a billion people made him the greatest deliverer of "goodness" in world history.

How did Deng Xiaoping decide to move a billion people? Change begins in the minds of men and women. After two traumatic centuries and a rich reservoir of feudal culture (which Mao had diminished but not eliminated), keeping China together would have been an achievement. But Deng wanted to catapult his billion people into the modern world, despite China's enormous historical disadvantages. He wanted to take the quickest short cut in history. He found the roadmap in America.

When Deng visited America in January 1979, he could have decided to use the absolute control he had over the Chinese media to carefully control the flow of information on his visit. Similarly, he could have chosen to restrict the flow of information on American society. Indeed, until Deng's visit, the Chinese had been fed a distorted view of American society through the state-controlled media. The images of America shared with the Chinese masses were all designed to reinforce the traditional propaganda that was being put out by all Communist parties, including the Chinese Communist Party, on America. In this propaganda, America was portrayed as a typical capitalist society where large numbers of the poor were exploited by a small, greedy exploitative class of capitalists and where the American people were routinely fleeced by their robber barons. The Chinese were told that China was lucky to have been spared this wretched fate.

Let me in parenthesis state that the Chinese leaders were not deceived themselves. Despite the absence of any direct contact between America and China before Henry Kissinger's famous secret visit to Beijing in July 1971, the Chinese leaders had a very informed and sophisticated view of American society and how it worked. One story is worth telling. In 1972, during the presidential elections campaign, the Chinese premier, Zhou En Lai (a legendary Chinese figure), received a bright young student from Oxford who was politically active. Her name was Benazir Bhutto, the daughter of one of Pakistan's leaders, Zulfikar Ali Bhutto. As Benazir had visited America often, Zhou En Lai asked her for her assessment of the U.S. presidential elections. Benazir Bhutto, pointing to the numerous anti-war protests in American campuses, confidently declared that McGovern would win. Zhou En Lai demurred. He proceeded to give the young lady a state-by-state analysis of the respective candidate's proposals and ended by confidently predicting that Richard Nixon would win by a landslide. This prediction came true. Zhou En Lai had not been to America. Benazir had. Yet, he showed a far more sophisticated understanding of American society.

Deng would have had the same sophisticated understanding of American society that Zhou did. Even before he went to America, he must have realized the gap between the Chinese Communist Party's negative portrayals of American society and the positive realities that he knew. He must have also known the political risks of demonstrating that the Chinese Communist Party's propaganda was false. This would have damaged both the credibility and legitimacy of the Communist Party, an instrument that he still needed to use to transform China.

Nevertheless, Deng decided to take a huge political risk and instructed the Chinese media to show (without any propagandistic overlay) how the American people actually lived. He allowed Chinese TV to show scenes of ordinary American homes, filled with items that were then way beyond Chinese dreams: refrigerators, washing machines, cars. In so doing, Deng shattered the Communist Party myth that the ordinary American people toiled in poverty and misery. He also made the Chinese acutely aware how backward their conditions were.

Deng knew exactly what he was doing. The Chinese Communist Party had had many achievements but one of its biggest achievements was to transform the industrious Chinese people into a non-industrious race. With the "iron rice bowl" provided by the Chinese Communist Party rule, there was no incentive to work hard. One of the longest haircuts I ever had was in Shanghai: The barber got paid the same whether he did one haircut or twenty haircuts in one day. I remember also leaving a hotel in Shanghai to try to catch a cab. There were over twenty cabs lined up. Each driver argued that it was not his turn to take a passenger. These were the everyday effects of the "iron rice bowl".

Deng decided to use the American dream to smash the "iron rice bowl." He told the Chinese people that they could prosper if they sought to work as hard as the Americans and accumulated individual wealth. He could have made these arguments logically and rationally. But it would have taken decades to work. Instead, he just showed the Chinese people how ordinary Americans lived. The sharing of the American dream provided the Chinese people with their critical ingredients for success: hope and motivation.

The TV exposure Deng allowed was not a one-off event. Throughout the 1980s and 1990s, one of the most popular programs on Chinese TV was a program entitled *One World*, which was produced by a beautiful American Chinese woman, Yue-Sai Kan. She showed many different aspects of American society to the Chinese. In so doing, she became a household name in China. Her own life then demonstrated the American success story. She went from being a TV producer to an entrepreneur, whose cosmetic products and Chinese Barbie-type dolls (Yue-Sai wa-wa, as they are called) have become enormously popular in China. Yue-Sai not only lived the American dream. In living it, she also exported it to China.

The three most important societies in Asia are probably China, India, and Japan. Remarkably, America has had a profound impact on the development of all three, but each in different ways. Deng decided to share the American dream with the Chinese people through a big-bang approach. This appears to have worked. The history of the Indo-American relationship is more complicated.

As the two largest democracies in the world, America and India should have naturally come together. However, the geopolitics of the Cold War got in the way. America leaned towards China and Pakistan to balance the Soviet Union. India was then forced to bend towards the Soviet Union to balance its rivals, China and Pakistan, two countries it had gone to war with. This geopolitical divide could have wrecked the Indo-American relationship for a long time.

Fortunately, India, unlike China, was not a closed society. First hundreds, later thousands, of Indians went to study in North American universities. Many stayed on in America. This led to a curious paradox. India remained one of the poorest societies on earth and seemed destined to remain so. By contrast, however, the Indians who studied and stayed in America became the most prosperous ethnic group in the most prosperous society on earth. It took a while for Indian society to become aware of this reality. But the high-tech boom in the 1990s suddenly created a few Indian billionaires and made both the Indians and the world aware that the Indians in America had engineered a remarkable success story.

This led to a new burst of hope among young Indians, who began to develop the cultural confidence that they were on par with the rest of the world. One of the most unforgettable memories of my life came from a visit to Bangalore in the early 1990s. One day, we arrived in a typical Indian street, dusty, packed with people, with vintage cars crawling along it; a typical Third World scene. We stopped at a door, walked up a flight of stairs and after passing through several air-conditioned rooms, we arrived at a state-of-the art modern computer room with the quiet buzz of a few software writers working away. I asked a young Indian what he was working on. He said that his "buddy" in California had just finished working on a software package. Before going to bed, his Californian buddy had sent all his "work-in-progress" to him in Bangalore so that this young Indian could keep working on this software package while California slept. In short, between the two of them in California and Bangalore, they maintained a twenty-four-hour operation, at state-of-the-art and first-world levels.

The electronic connection between California and Bangalore delivered more than software bits. Culture was also transmitted. It made the people of Bangalore, and later the people of India, aware that they could work and achieve first-world standards. Imagine the revolutionary impact of the American ethos on a social fabric that deeply believed that destiny was set at birth. American society is inherently meritocratic. Indian society had never been so. The British colonial rulers may have introduced a few drops of meritocracy, but they never expected the natives of India to believe that they were culturally or intellectually on par with, or heaven forbid, superior to their British rulers. Americans, by contrast, celebrated the achievements of their Indian counterparts and happily accepted them as equals.

India is about to make a big leap into the modern world. A major renaissance is about to take place, fueled by various economic success stories. How a society or culture turns away from stagnation to a burst of creative development is a complex story. But when the verdict of history is written from a clearer perspective a century from now, it will show that the American spreading of a culture of meritocracy played a key role in liberating the Indian mindset and convincing Indian society that it could successfully compete in the modern world on equal terms. The cultural osmosis with America has played a key role in changing the Indian mindset. When India succeeds, it should send America a big thank-you note. But Indian gratitude is alive. Even though reservoirs of goodwill towards America are diminishing in many parts of the world, the reservoir in India remains strong and is likely to remain so for decades to come.

It is still too early to tell whether the twenty-first century will resemble more the troubled first half of the twentieth century (which experienced two disastrous world wars) or the second half of the twentieth century (which, despite the Cold War, saw massive improvements in the standard of living in many parts of the world). But it is not too early to assess which factors will lead to stability or instability.

One of the most powerful stabilizing forces in the world is the emergence of pools of middle-class citizens in many societies around the world. Their world views may be conditioned both by their culture and geography but increasingly their material aspirations have begun to resemble those of middle-class Americans: a rewarding and fulfilling job, a comfortable home, education for their children and a better future for them, and the ability to live according to ideals and beliefs they choose for themselves. The American middle class has demonstrated the many virtues that flow out of such aspirations. Many societies now just want to copy America.

Deng Xiaoping was once asked whether he was hopeful about China's future. His reply (or so I am told) was, "Just wait till the 40,000 Chinese students return from American universities. That's when real change will come." When societies began to replicate the American middle class they also (almost by a process of osmosis) began to absorb many of the values that underpin this social strata: a belief in a secular social order (where citizens, not established hierarchical authorities, make the key decisions); a belief in the value of scientific inquiry and consequent willingness to challenge conventional wisdom; and a belief that each individual has a capacity to make a contribution to developing a better society. None of these values are consciously articulated. Nor are they taught explicitly. But the great belief in progress that the West developed over the course of the past few centuries and which America probably perfected in the latter half of the twentieth century has now been shared with middle-class communities around the world. The greater the number of individuals around the world who share the American belief that the world can be a better place, the greater the likelihood that the world is headed for more stability. This is no small contribution by America to the world.

Given the remarkable historical contribution that America as a society has made to other societies, it is hard to imagine how world history would have turned out if America had not been born. It is conceivable that in the late twentieth and early twenty-first centuries, our world could have still continued with the zero-sum games that nations played with each other. Whenever one nation became powerful, it felt almost an obligation to expand, dominate, or conquer its neighbors. This strain of behavior had been almost genetically imprinted into every nation of the world.

Perhaps America's greatest contribution may have been to smash the natural continuation of this age-old tendency. In 1945, at the peak of its power, America decided to create a rules-based order that would allow any nation to flourish. Neither Truman nor Eleanor Roosevelt believed that they were putting in place an order that would ensure continued American hegemony over the world. They assumed, as most Americans did, that America would do well under any condition. They had great faith, as most Americans did, in the inherent vibrancy of American society. Strength and confidence begets generosity. The generosity of the American spirit clearly shows through the arrangements America made for the world order in 1945.

This generous attitude of the American government towards the rest of the world also reflected the generous attitude of individual Americans towards the world. Indeed, the best face of America emerges when individual Americans meet individual foreigners. Hence when the density of face-to-face contacts increases with Americans, the inevitable result seems to be an accumulation of goodwill towards America.

These days, one of the most common facilitators of face-to-face interaction between Americans and others around the world is humanitarian-assistance groups. Many individual Americans participate with such groups overseas, helping crisis-stricken areas to rebuild and providing food and healthcare to those in need. Locals who have contact with such Americans often come away with great affection and respect for their foreign helpers. Following the December 26, 2003, earthquake in Bam, a city in southern Iran, several teams of humanitarian-assistance workers went to aid the city's recovery. Many of these workers were Americans, and they encountered tremendous goodwill from the people of Iran, a country that has experienced a troubled history with America.

Indeed, Iranian goodwill goes far beyond mere thanks for humanitarian relief. Following a trip to Tehran, Elie Krakowski described how Iranians from all walks of life shared a deep fondness for America: "What I encountered . . . was not just pleasantness and friendliness, but strongly pro-American feelings, expressed enthusiastically." One Iranian shopkeeper vibrantly described "how nice Americans were, how much Iranians looked back fondly on the times when Americans regularly came to Iran, and how much he and others were hoping those days would return." [4]

That shopkeeper wasn't referring to American aid workers, but to normal everyday Americans. While skeptics might easily brush aside gratitude and goodwill in areas of crisis where humanitarian workers are representing their countries, the real source of goodwill towards Americans comes from daily interactions between ordinary people.

A good friend of mine in Singapore, Koh Boon Hwee, tells a remarkable story. At the age of eighteen, during school vacation, he worked for an American manager, William H. Schroeder, as a key-punch operator (in the days when computers ran on cards that had to be individually punched). Koh Boon Hwee did well. In the space of three months, his salary quadrupled because he went from card punch operator to 360 application systems programmer. As the going was good, Koh Boon Hwee told his American manager that since he was being treated so well, he was entertaining the idea of continuing work and not going to college to take an engineering course. The reaction of the American manager was swift and decisive. He said that he would immediately sack Koh Boon Hwee if he decided not to go to college. The American manager was more concerned over the long-term personal future of Koh Boon Hwee than he was over losing a valuable employee. Koh Boon Hwee went on to do very well, thanks to the inspiring generosity of his American manager. This American manager also personally paid for the college education of several young Singaporeans, including the sons of his Chinese Singaporean housekeeper.

I too have encountered similar American generosity. In 1968, when I was twenty years old, I shared with a fellow student, Dean Swift, an American from Colorado, my dream of visiting the Himalayas someday. Dean had come to Singapore for a one-year visiting study program. He did *not* come from a rich family. He had seen my family's home in Singapore, when we were paying US$6 a month for rental in a rent-controlled pre-war home. He knew that I could not afford to travel. Within weeks, Dean produced $2,000 in U.S. money, gave it to me and said that I should go visit the Himalayas. We remain friends to this day.

Indeed, virtually all the Americans that I met in Singapore and Asia in the first few decades of my life displayed this same generosity to fellow human beings whom they knew to be disadvantaged. At the height of the Vietnam War, when American public sentiment was overwhelmingly anti-war and the American soldiers were portrayed in the American media in less than heroic terms, I was struck by the openness and generosity of the few American GIs who came to Singapore for rest and recreation. The American anti-war protestors I met in Southeast Asia were no less generous. Both the pro-war and anti-war Americans I met shared the same generosity of spirit.

This explains a particularly counterintuitive fact. America dropped over 7 million tons of bombs in Vietnam (as opposed to only 2 million in World War II); it also killed hundreds of thousands of Vietnamese in brutal battles. The natural result of all this when the United States pulled out in 1973 and the war ended in 1975 should have been to leave behind a huge reservoir of hate in Vietnam. Instead, almost from the very first day after the war ended, Americans could walk safely on the streets of Vietnam. The Vietnamese people do not hate the Americans. Indeed, at a time when Americans are increasingly feeling unloved and threatened, one of the safest places in the world for an American to visit is Vietnam. Despite having fought a brutal war in Vietnam, America has left behind in Vietnam a huge reservoir of goodwill.

How could this have happened? Only a Vietnamese can explain this unnatural phenomenon fully. But let me venture a simple theory. Most individual Americans tend to be generous souls. They seem to have a natural instinct to help the underdog. Through the Vietnam War, millions of Vietnamese and millions of Americans dealt closely with each other face-to-face. At the nation-to-nation level, the North Vietnamese government successfully demonized the American government. But at the face-to-face level, the Vietnamese encountered many generous and kind Americans who certainly did not show them contempt. Many Vietnamese may have been puzzled by the naiveté of the Americans they met. But they could see clearly that most came with good intentions, to help and not to destroy Vietnam.

The recent Iraq war has in some ways reignited some of the political battles over the Vietnam War. Many who oppose the American intervention in Iraq said that this was the beginning of a new "Vietnam," where America would once again be trapped in a quagmire and would end up alienating the population of the country. Eventually, the price in American lives would be too high and America would once again have to leave ignominiously.

No one can rule this out from happening. Curiously in all this debate about Iraq becoming another "Vietnam," few commentators have noticed that Vietnam has quietly assisted America in Iraq. It may have only provided some small assistance in the form of shipments of rice. The contribution was clearly symbolic, but it was a very powerful symbol. The country that came to assist America in its new "Vietnam" was Vietnam.

~ 2 ~

How America Has Harmed
the World

A T THE END OF THE COLD WAR, America made an awesome strategic error: It decided to behave like an ordinary country. There is nothing inherently wrong with behaving like an ordinary country, especially a peaceful ordinary country. The only problem is that over the course of two hundred years, America had succeeded in convincing mankind that it was an extraordinary country. It had demonstrated this both in word and deed. Indeed nothing captured better the willingness of America to do good for the world than the famous and enduring words of President John F. Kennedy: "Let every nation know, whether it wishes us well or ill, that we shall pay any price, bear any burden, meet any hardship, support any friend, oppose any foe, in order to assure the survival and the success of liberty." These were his words in his inaugural address of January 20, 1961.

The end of the Cold War was therefore a unique moment in America's relations with the world. It was at the peak of its moral authority. Almost all countries looked up to America. And, as the previous chapter has documented, America had accumulated enormous reservoirs of goodwill around the world. With so much accumulated moral authority and political goodwill, America could have done so much more for the world. Instead, it chose effectively to retreat and disengage from the world, especially from many of the burdensome commitments it made during the Cold War.

America never intended to do any harm. But the process of disengagement proved to be a wrenching and painful experience for many countries in the world. Over the course of previous decades, many of these countries had thickened their relations with America. Some of this thickening was a natural result of the growing global interdependence flowing from the various forces of globalization that America had unleashed. The fundamental message that America had sent to the world was: Open up your economies, integrate yourself with the world, and you will prosper. America would guarantee the continuation of a global order that would allow nations to flourish. This was the implicit social contract between America and its friends in the world.

It will take decades before we understand why America decided to behave like a normal country when the Cold War ended. Perhaps it was due to the exhaustion of having spent four decades competing with the Soviet Union globally. Some of my American friends have described to me vividly how personally relieved they felt to learn that the nuclear nightmare that they had been living with for decades had finally disappeared. With that nightmare over, they only wanted to return to a happy normal life. The burdens of the world had become too heavy to carry.

However, it will not take decades to understand the consequences of America's post–Cold War decision to behave like a normal country. Many countries suffered directly or indirectly as a result of the American process of disengagement. What is even more troubling is the possibility that perhaps the events of 9/11 had their origins in this American decision to walk away from the world, and to walk away (without thinking through the consequences) from countries with which America had developed close relations.

Pakistan probably provides the best example of what can go wrong when disengagement is done thoughtlessly. Today, there is no country that Western policymakers worry more about than Pakistan, a nuclear-weapons state whose long-term political stability appears uncertain. The danger of a breakdown of state control over the nuclear weapons of Pakistan is not an abstract or theoretical worry. The worry is real because in early 2004, Pakistan both exposed and took disciplinary action against the "father" of Pakistan's nuclear program, A Q Khan, for having illegally sold nuclear technology to Libya and North Korea. Yet all this leakage of nuclear technology happened when Pakistan had a strong central government. Any political instability in Pakistan leading to a weaker government would inevitably provide greater opportunities for leakage of either nuclear technology or critical nuclear components in a world where there are well-financed terrorist organizations looking for the perfect "dirty bomb" to use in crowded major cities.

Given the enormous stakes that the whole world, including America, have in Pakistan's long-term political stability, it will come as a surprise to many Americans to learn that the one country that has done a lot to destabilize Pakistan in recent decades has been America. During the Cold War, Pakistan was considered a key ally of America. Most Americans, including senior policymakers, have vague memories of cooperation with Pakistan then. Most Pakistanis, especially senior policymakers, have vivid memories of their many contributions during the Cold War: from facilitating the "secret" visit of Henry Kissinger to China in 1971 (for which China still remains grateful to Pakistan) to providing all the logistics and support to channel American money and arms to the Islamic mujahideen fighting the Soviet occupation of Afghanistan in the 1980s. During this war, every major American figure wanted to go to Pakistan, travel to Peshawar, and have a photo-op at the mountainous border between Afghanistan and Pakistan, a border that was depicted as the front line in the battle to defend freedom.

When the Cold War ended, this once-precious border was deemed to be strategically irrelevant by Washington policymakers. Pakistan was quietly dropped as an ally. American aid was curtailed or frozen. Not surprisingly, the Pakistanis have a deep sense of betrayal: seduced, used and abandoned, is how they perceive the history of their relations with America.

Some American policymakers may dismiss the Pakistani claim that they were used and abandoned. They would argue that the Pakistani elite were not born yesterday. The Pakistani elite were worldly wise and knew the ways of the world. All such alliances between states are purely cynical and tactical bargains where each side uses the other for mutual gain. When the job of destroying the Soviet empire was done, Pakistan had served its usefulness and the contract was over. This is how the real world is run. True! The only problem here is that America does not want to be perceived as a cynical ordinary country. America believes that it represents a more principled state, not a petty, scheming Machiavellian operation.

Herein lies the nub of the problem. Like any other state, America wants to have the freedom to engage in cynical deeds for short-term gains. However, unlike any other state, it does not want to be perceived as a cynical actor motivated by realpolitik. It wants to be viewed and respected as a country that stands by certain values and that is constantly trying to develop a political order based on certain principles. This is what America proclaimed that it stood for during and after the Cold War.

After the Cold War ended, the visions expressed by both President George H. W. Bush and President Bill Clinton were similar. When President George H. W. Bush declared that a New World Order was being born with the end of the Cold War and the success of the Gulf War, he reached into the best Wilsonian traditions of American foreign policy to describe the new world:

> We have a vision of a new partnership of nations that transcends the Cold War. A partnership based on consultation, cooperation, and collective action, especially through international and regional organizations. A partnership united by principle and the rule of law and supported by an equitable sharing of both cost and commitment. A partnership whose goals are to increase democracy, increase prosperity, increase the peace, and reduce arms.[1]

This Wilsonian rhetoric continued after Clinton's Democratic administration replaced Bush's Republican administration. Americans may not take the rhetoric of their presidents seriously. But the rest of the world does. President Clinton spoke in almost Kennedy-esque terms when he said that America's goals in the world exceeded its narrow national interests. He said America had a larger goal of expanding democracy and the free world. "In a new era of peril and opportunity, our overriding purpose must be to expand and strengthen the world's community of market-based democracies. During the Cold War, we sought to contain a threat to survival of free institutions. Now we seek to enlarge the circle of nations that live under those free institutions, for our dream is of a day when the opinions and energies of every person in the world will be given full expression in a world of thriving democracies that cooperate with each other and live in peace."[2]

Try to imagine the reaction of any sophisticated Pakistani as he heard these words. He would have noted that the speech spoke of a dream of "a day when the opinions and energies of every person in the world will be given full expression in a world of thriving democracies that cooperate with each other and live in peace." He would face two problems with this statement. Firstly, he would be skeptical of the claim that America cared about "every person in the world." The Pakistani people were dropped by America with no thought given to the consequences they might face. Secondly, he would question America's commitment to promoting democracy.

The record of America's relationship with Pakistan showed that America only promoted democracy in Pakistan when American national interests were not at stake (in the mid-1990s when Pakistan served no real purpose for America). However, when Pakistan began to matter to American national interests, America worked happily with military governments, indeed preferring them, while paying lip service to the need for democracy. America has declared that it promotes democracy only to help other people, not itself. But the record with Pakistan (and with quite a few other states critical to American national interests) shows that America will only promote democracy if it does not harm American national interests.

Pakistan is a unique state in many ways. It is both fragile as well as strong. Its fragility comes from its large poor population, whose standard of living has not improved much in recent years. They therefore provide a potential large pool of recruits for radical Islamic causes. Indeed, in the decade that America turned away from Pakistan, the number of Madrasahs (the traditional Islamic schools) had more than doubled, rising to upwards of 45,000. Yet, it is also a strong state because it has a strong state structure, a strong military establishment, and a sophisticated elite that has been educated in leading universities, including many in North America. The leading Pakistani minds passing judgment on America are extremely intelligent and sophisticated.

It would be fascinating to step into those minds to learn what they think of the new partnership that has been forged between America and Pakistan to fight Osama bin Laden and Al-Qaeda post–9/11. Indeed, following Secretary of State Colin Powell's visit to Pakistan in March 2004, Pakistan was given the status of "Major Non-NATO Ally" (MNNA). Superficially, things between America and Pakistan seem to be going on truly well. But any Pakistani viewing this "second" partnership with America must view it through the prism of the "first" partnership during the Cold War. Then a close relationship of trust and confidence had been built between the Pakistani and American foreign-policy and security establishments. Today, any senior Pakistani who advocates a similar rebuilding of trust would probably be cashiered immediately. Instead, the voices likely to receive more attention are those who say "Last time, they used us and dropped us. Let's see who's going to be the sucker now." Tragically, through its post–Cold War behavior towards Pakistan, America has given Pakistan an incentive to cooperate, but not too much. It does not serve Pakistan's interest to see the battle against Osama bin Laden end with a swift decisive victory. If this happens, Pakistan would once again become less relevant to American interests (although the presence of nuclear weaponry will now always provide strong incentives for America to pursue stability in Pakistan).

This is the real cost of the breakdown in trust and confidence between the American and Pakistani establishments. America has demonstrated that it is an unreliable ally. Hence, in the new, perhaps much more dangerous struggle against radical Islamic groups who use terrorism as a weapon, America will have a much harder time convincing Pakistan that it will stay the course: that it won't use it and abandon it again. Without complete Pakistani support, it will be difficult to solve the problem in Afghanistan, where indeed the planning for 9/11 was carried out.

Just as most Americans are ignorant of the recent history of Pakistani-American relations, they are also unaware of the legacy America left behind in Afghanistan at the end of the Cold War. Without understanding this legacy, it will be difficult for America to find a lasting solution for Afghanistan. Osama bin Laden initially rode to power and success in Afghanistan with strong American support. In an effort both to bleed the Soviets in Afghanistan and to eventually dislodge them, America was happy to support, financially and materially, all the Muslims from all over the world who were willing to come to Afghanistan to fight the Soviet infidels.

"Between 1978 and 1992, the U.S. government poured at least $6 billion (some estimates range as high as $20 billion) worth of arms, training and funds to prop up the mujaheddin factions. Other Western governments, as well as oil-rich Saudi Arabia, kicked in as much again. Wealthy Arab fanatics, like Osama bin Laden, provided millions more." This foreign funding powered several training camps in Afghanistan, camps that taught established mujaheddin and interested foreign volunteers alike skills such as sabotage and urban terrorism. Osama bin Laden's career path put him in charge of Maktab al Khidamar, the organization that oversaw distribution of "recruits, money and equipment . . . to the mujaheddin."[3] From there it was only a matter of unofficially returning to his former post in the 1990s, once he had grown disillusioned with the United States after the Gulf War. This is how a Saudi national, whose family had accumulated a fortune of several billion dollars, came to Afghanistan to fight the Soviets.

There is nothing natural about a Saudi citizen going to Afghanistan to fight the Soviets. It would be as unnatural as a Brazilian going to Mexico to fight, say, an American occupation of Mexico's Baja California. The Brazilians and Mexicans do not speak the same language. The only thing that unites them is that they are nominally Catholic. The Saudis and Afghans also do not speak the same language. The historic and cultural gulf between them is greater than that which divides Brazil and Mexico. The only thing that united the Saudis and Afghans was their belief in Islam. But if a nineteenth-century Saudi citizen had been asked to go to Afghanistan to defend his fellow Muslim brothers from the perfidious British invasion of Afghanistan in 1839, the Saudi would have looked puzzled. He would have probably replied: "But the Afghans are not even Arabs!"

Hence, in enthusiastically trying to whip up Islamic sentiment against the Soviet invasion of Afghanistan, America may have inadvertently woken up a sleeping dragon of Islamic solidarity that had remained latent and buried for centuries. Napoleon once famously remarked, "Let China sleep, for when she wakes, she will shake the world." Napoleon could just as easily have made the same remarks about the Islamic world. When this world was in deep sleep, European colonizers freely roamed there and trampled Islamic societies under their boots. Little did they fear that they would stir up powerful forces in the Islamic world. One of the great historical ironies here is that what the brutal European colonizers failed to do in the Islamic world in a century, America has managed to do in a decade.

America and Islam are two societies that have had, for the most part, minimal historical connections and which, following the logic of history and geography, should have had no reason to move into a position of natural opposition. Most Americans don't understand the contemporary Islamic anger against them. They believe that they are completely innocent. It comes as a shock to most American citizens to be told that their government may have, knowingly or not, radicalized Islam. But that is what happened in the 1990s. The extent to which America has already stirred the Islamic world explains why finding a long-term solution is proving such an intractable challenge.

It was perhaps no accident that the plot to demolish the World Trade Center, the Pentagon and, probably, the White House was planned in Afghanistan. Afghanistan had provided American poli-cymakers with one of their sweetest victories since World War II when in 1989 the massive Soviet empire was brought to its knees and forced to undertake an ignominious withdrawal. What made it truly sweet was that all this was accomplished without the loss of a single American soldier. All that America had to do was to rally the Afghan warriors and strengthen them by sending in heavily armed Islamic mujahideen from all over the world. American technology played a vital role. The powerful Soviet aircraft and helicopters be-came sitting ducks in the Afghan mountains and valleys when the Islamic mujahideen were armed with American Stinger missiles. The motivation to fight was provided by the teachings of a seventh-century prophet; the ability to fight was provided by twentieth-cen-tury American technology. This was a powerful combination. America created it.

One of the greatest warriors in the battle against the Soviet occu-pation was Ahmad Shah Massoud (who was tragically killed by Osama bin Laden just before 9/11). Massoud famously remarked once: "There are only two things the Afghans must have: the Koran and the Stinger."[4]

Ahmed Rashid, a Pakistani journalist, is widely reputed to be the most astute observer of Afghanistan. In a review of a book on the CIA's role in Afghanistan, he said:

> . . . The CIA particularly encouraged the recruitment of radical Islamist fighters—many of whom were linked to the Muslim Brotherhood—believing them to be more dedicated to the defeat of the Soviet occupying forces than secular or royalist Afghani groups. As Coll writes, the United States adopted a policy that looked forward to a new era of direct infusions of advanced U.S. military technology into Afghanistan, intensified training of Is-lamist guerrillas in explosives and sabotage techniques, and tar-

geted attacks on Soviet military officers designed to demoralize the Soviet high command. Among other consequences these changes pushed the CIA, along with its clients in the Afghan resistance and in Pakistani intelligence, closer to the gray fields of assassination and terrorism."[5]

In the same review, Ahmed Rashid added: "Condoleezza Rice almost inadvertently summed up the dilemma of both the Clinton and the Bush administrations when she testified before the September 11 commission on April 8:

America's al-Qaeda policy wasn't working because our Afghanistan policy wasn't working. And our Afghanistan policy wasn't working because our Pakistan policy wasn't working . . .

But this recognition by Condoleezza Rice came in April 2004.

In 1990, after having launched a powerful new force in world history, America decided that it could safely walk away from it and go home. What America left behind in Afghanistan was a vacuum. It would be useful to discover whether the American government officials in charge of the policy towards Afghanistan then gave any thought to the consequences that would flow from leaving behind the vacuum. Alas, the archives of the American government from that period are not open yet. It is impossible to tell whether any American policymaker speculated about the obvious consequences that would flow from the creation of a political vacuum in Afghanistan. As in nature, other forces would enter to fill the political vacuum. In practice, a combination of forces coalesced to create the Taleban government: domestic dissatisfaction with corrupt warlords left behind by America, Saudi money, Osama bin Laden's active involvement, and the desire of the Pakistani intelligence service to protect their strategic flanks by creating a regime favorably disposed to Pakistan. America did not approve of the arrival of the Taleban regime but it saw no direct danger to America. A policy of benign neglect fell into place. Afghanistan thus became a strategic orphan in the 1990s.

Any American who has a deep desire to understand the root causes of 9/11 should begin by studying carefully the recent history of Afghanistan and the many ways in which America has walked into Afghan history. American policies have made huge differences to lives all across the planet but often the right hand of America is not aware what the left hand is doing. Afghanistan provides a classic example of how different hands of America work at cross-purposes. The *political* hand of America decided that at the end of the Cold War, Afghanistan had to be abandoned even if Afghanistan fell into chaos. No vital short-term American interests were at stake. In the same period, the *economic* hand of America continued to accelerate the pace of globalization, creating a borderless world, shrinking the globe, leading to a literal disappearance of distance. The politics of America allowed chaos to be created in Afghanistan; the economics of America drew the chaos closer to America. These were, in simple terms, the origins of the catastrophe that occurred in September 2001.

Many Americans would like to believe that the anger that led to 9/11 was at best an "unintended consequence" of some American actions. But a point that this book will argue repeatedly is that many "unintended consequences" are actually "intended consequences." The consequences of a shrinking globe are simple and obvious. While there were once different pools of history that were connected either indirectly or marginally, even in the heyday of European colonial expansion around the globe, today American policies and American technology have effectively created a broadband connection that has rapidly accelerated the movements between the different pools of history.

America did not "intend" to wake up the radical forces in the Islamic world when it stirred up Islamic solidarity against the Soviet invasion of Afghanistan. Nor did it "intend" to bring the pools of chaos closer to America when it unleashed the forces of globalization across the planet. But in trying to understand how the world needs to be managed in the twenty-first century, it is vital that American policymakers first liberate themselves from their belief that they should only be judged by their intentions, not the consequence of their actions.

The rest of the world does not "see" American intentions. It only experiences the many complex effects of American actions. If American policymakers refuse to either understand or accept responsibility for the natural consequences of their actions, they will increasingly be resented around the planet. Anti-Americanism will rise. Two British writers, Ziauddin Sarder and Merryl Wyn Davies, in an effort to explain the rise of anti-Americanism, have made this point.

> One of the main points we make in this book is that many of the worst effects of American power are the result of the best-intentioned actions. As a result, the animosity in other parts of the world often seems unaccountable to the U.S., and this makes it difficult for well-meaning Americans to conceive of an effective change in policy.[6]

Unless American society is determined to understand its impact on the rest of the world, a vicious circle is likely to ensue. Virtually all American decisions, both domestic and international, have an impact on the rest of the world. This is an inevitable consequence of American power and the huge American success with globalization. But even as American actions continue to intrude into the lives of other citizens with increasing force, Americans continue to display either ignorance that their actions impact others or puzzlement that the impact causes resentment. This display of ignorance and puzzlement further aggravates the resentment.

The enormous tragic consequences that have flowed from the strategic American decision to walk away thoughtlessly from Pakistan and Afghanistan should provide ample proof of the opening argument of this chapter that America made an awesome strategic error when it decided to behave like a normal country. But these were not the only countries that felt abandoned by America in the 1990s. Several other nations felt equally abandoned but each was abandoned in its own way. Each had some reasons to believe that it had developed a special relationship with America. But when it came to face a crisis, America reacted as though no such relationship existed. It is hard to keep count of the countries who have felt in one way or another betrayed by America. Till today, most Americans remain unaware of this.

Apart from economics students and some financiers who lost their shirts over it, few Americans have a strong memory of the Asian financial crisis of 1997. It began with a sudden loss of confidence in the Thai currency, the baht. Several hedge funds speculated against the baht and, after losing billions of dollars trying to defend its currency, the Thai government gave up and devalued. Initially, this was seen as an isolated event. Indonesia, then governed by President Suharto, offered to help Thailand with a loan of US$500 million. But the loss of confidence in the Thai baht soon spread to the Malaysian ringgit and the Indonesian rupiah. The Southeast Asian currencies, with the exception of the strongly backed Singapore dollar, began to fall like dominoes.

The International Monetary Fund tried to help. Its intention was to make things better. With the benefit of hindsight, it is becoming clearer that the "cookie cutter" solutions (devised by the IMF in response to crises in Latin America) may have made things worse in

Southeast Asia. In fact, it is now clear that many of the IMF's conditions for relief loans were impractical and even hazardous to the developing countries. This is how Rick Rowden described the record of the IMF and the World Bank:

> Much of the rhetoric about "institutions" and "best practices" heard coming from the IMF and World Bank in the development loan conditions also doesn't fit with the history. When the rich countries were developing over the last few centuries, they largely lacked such basics as universal suffrage, modern bureaucracies, enforcement of intellectual property rights laws, corporate governance laws and regulations such as bankruptcy laws and competition laws, and even central banks and securities regulations. The rich countries developed these institutions much later in their industrialization processes than many of us might think; yet here too, the IMF and World Bank insist that it is the lack of such institutions which explains why the poor countries have not yet successfully developed. In fact, the history suggests that these institutions were more the result of, rather than prerequisites for, successful industrialization.[7]

Consequently, those who followed the IMF advice, like Thailand and Indonesia, fared badly. Malaysia defied the conventional wisdom and imposed currency controls. It survived the financial crisis and indeed bounced back. Joseph Stiglitz has given as good an account as anyone else of the IMF record in the Asian financial crisis in his book *Globalization and Its Discontents*. While the book was criticized by some economists, his arguments have found some resonance in Asia.

Many Asians also remember the crucial decisions that were made by the U.S. Treasury during the Asian financial crisis. None of these decisions were taken with any explicit intention of harming the Asian economies, but nonetheless a lot of damage was done by them. A few in particular stood out. First, when Thailand began to reel under the attack on the baht, the U.S. Treasury had to make a crucial decision on whether or not to intervene to help the Thai currency. When Mexico had faced similar crises in 1982 and 1994, the U.S. Treasury intervened strongly and powerfully to defend the peso, both directly and indirectly. Massive loans were offered to Mexico, together with direct phone calls to leading American banks urging them not to call on loans provided to Mexico. These direct interventions made sense. Any unrest or instability in Mexico would spill over into the United States. Hence, in helping Mexico, America was only protecting itself.

An astute American journalist, Tom Plate, wrote a column in the *Los Angeles Times* on July 22, 1997, entitled, "Will Washington do for the free-falling Baht what it did for the Mexican Peso? Don't bank on it." In this column, he said, "I asked a Washington official why the U.S. rode to the rescue of Mexico but not of Thailand. There was a chuckle and then this: 'Thailand's not on our border.'" Over a year later, in another column in the *Los Angeles Times* on October 6, 1998, he identified this U.S. Treasury official as Lawrence Summers, then the deputy treasury secretary. Summers may have been unusually candid in his remarks but what he said was clearly obvious to any observer.

Thailand had been a strong and firm ally of the United States throughout the Cold War, serving as a SEATO member and providing the air bases for the conduct of the air war against Vietnam. The strong links between the Thai royal family, which remains enormously influential, and American society pre-dated the Cold War. Over the years, the Thai establishment was happy to be perceived as one of America's best friends in Southeast Asia. And Thai leaders were received as such when they visited Washington, D.C.

Many Thais therefore felt a sense of betrayal when the U.S. Treasury decided that Thailand, unlike Mexico, did not have sufficient strategic importance to merit direct American assistance. The Thais felt that they were left twisting in the wind as a storm surged around them. What made them feel even more aggrieved was their realization that one reason that the financial crisis had befallen them was that they had heeded American policymakers' advice to liberalize their financial flows. Countries that had not heeded this American advice, like China and India, weathered the currency crisis well. Countries like Thailand that had followed the U.S. Treasury's advice suffered.

The Indonesian establishment felt a similar sense of betrayal. Indonesia, unlike Thailand, was never formally an American ally. But during the Cold War, when America and the Soviet Union competed ferociously for influence in the Third World, Indonesia was seen as a prize catch by the United States. President Suharto ruled from 1967 to 1998, with strong American support throughout most of his rule, despite private misgivings about his authoritarianism, corruption, and invasion of East Timor. American strategic priorities in having a country of 200 million on its side in the Cold War overrode all these misgivings. But it should also be noted that President Suharto's rule brought enormous benefits for the Indonesian people: the Food and Agriculture Organisation, the key U.N. body on agricultural issues, gave President Suharto an award in 1984 for his enormous success in transforming the once-starving Indonesia into a self-sufficient rice producer. Thus the American policy of supporting President Suharto had brought both strategic dividends and was perceived as having helped the Indonesian people, especially those at the very bottom of the economic ladder. English utilitarian philosophers would have approved.

When the Asian financial crisis broke out in 1997, President Suharto must have been comforted by the belief that Washington would help him out. For more than thirty years, America had invested a great deal of political capital in supporting him. He genuinely believed that he had become indispensable to American regional interests. But President Suharto, like most Americans, was unaware of the big U-turn in American policy: his country, once prized as a strategic asset, was now deemed a liability.

President Suharto was never explicitly told that U.S. policy towards him had changed. But as the crisis deepened and as the IMF continued to impose stringent demands in return for assistance, President Suharto became bewildered. At home, he was burdened by the demands of his family that he support their corruptly acquired business enterprises. His family's corruption had become deeply entrenched and had begun to eat away at the regime's legitimacy. The demise of the Suharto regime was a result of both internal rot and American decisions.

But there can be no doubt that the tipping point that led to the removal of President Suharto in 1998 was a result of a decision made by American policymakers. And when they made the decision, they neither looked at the big picture nor thought about the long-term consequences. Fareed Zakaria described well the thoughtlessness behind American policy towards Indonesia then:

Although they were not entirely to blame, the IMF and the U.S. government demanded immediate and radical reforms in Indonesia during its 1998 crisis, thereby helping delegitimatize and topple the government. Had they recognized the political instability these reforms would produce, they might have moderated their demands and made do with a more incremental approach. Suharto was running a flawed regime but one that had achieved order, secularism, and economic liberalization—an impressive combination in the Third World. Most important, nothing better was available to replace it. Gradual political reform rather than wholesale revolution would have been preferable, certainly for the average Indonesian, who one assumes was the intended beneficiary of Western policies.[8]

Since the removal of President Suharto, Indonesia has experienced a great deal of political instability and trauma. In the course of five years, Indonesia had three different Presidents: Habibie, Abdulrahman Wahid and Megawati Sukarnoputri. The economy, at its worst, shrank by 13.7 percent. In 1998, inflation soared to over 70 percent. The fifty million to a hundred million people at the bottom that Suharto had begun to lift out of poverty fell back into the poverty trap. In this cauldron of political and economic unrest, a democratic experiment was encouraged by America.

It is too early to tell how this democratic experiment will work out. Over time, President Megawati or her successor could play the role that President Putin has played in Russia and stabilize the situation. But this will not erase the effects of the political and economic trauma experienced by Indonesia as a result of sudden democratization in the midst of recession. America may have also inadvertently triggered the strong emergence of Islamic forces in Indonesia. Hence, the record may well show that just as the American abandonment of Afghanistan paved the way for 9/11/01, the American abandonment of the Suharto regime may have paved the way for 10/12/02. This was the date of the devastating bombing of a Bali nightclub that killed 88 Australians and 38 Indonesians. This had the same traumatic effect on Australia as 9/11 had on America. American actions have profound consequences.

When the Asian financial crisis spread to South Korea, it became apparent that America had made calculated decisions not to rescue Thailand and Indonesia. In South Korea, America had more direct interests. There were 37,000 American soldiers stationed along one of the most tense borders in the world, the Demilitarized Zone between South and North Korea. South Korea was also a major economy. Its collapse would have had wider global repercussions, possibly impacting the United States directly. Hence the U.S. Treasury decided to intervene forcefully. It worked with the IMF to raise a US$57 billion rescue package. It also worked the phones and told the major banks not to call in the loans to South Korea. In so doing, America sent a clear message that South Korea mattered. An equally clear message was sent that Thailand and Indonesia did not matter.

A curious episode during the Asian financial crisis also left many Asians puzzled about American intentions towards Asia. At the height of the crisis, Japan, the economic superpower of the region, offered to help by raising a $100 billion loan package. Japan had the resources to pull it off. However, America (which had then and still does have enormous political leverage over Japan, a dependent ally) intervened forcefully and vetoed any unilateral Japanese effort to help its fellow Asians. The message that America sent to the distressed Asian countries was a doubly unfortunate one. It said: "Not only will we not help you. We will also not let others help you."

One of America's biggest strengths is that it is a nation with limited memories. Unlike Europe, it is not burdened by the past. Asians, by contrast, have long memories. They can recall important historical events. The Asian financial crisis will be remembered for a long time. The lessons will be complex. It would be dangerous to oversimplify them. But one clear strand will emerge in the historical memory: how a once generous country walked away from them in their hour of need.

Such a memory is unlikely to exist in the American geostrategic consciousness. American policy horizons are determined by the framework of the four-year political cycle. Hence, when an administration, like the Clinton administration, is washed away from the offices of power, its accomplishments and sins are also seen to be washed away. Each new administration is seen to begin a new chapter in history. No contemporary administration wants to be held accountable for the sins of its predecessor. Americans feel a cleansing process when they flush an administration down into the sluices of history.

The rest of the world does not experience such a cleansing process. Other countries do not hold one single administration accountable. Instead they hold America accountable. This leads to a dangerous divide between America and the rest of the world. If there are mistakes made by an administration in its foreign policies, American voters blame the administration that acted on their behalf. This unwillingness to assume responsibility for their government's actions puzzles the rest of the world. America is the world's greatest democracy. All American administrations are elected or re-elected by the people. Surely ultimate responsibility or accountability for the actions of the administration must rest with the citizens of America?

In discussing the divide between how Americans view themselves vis-à-vis the rest of the world and how the rest of the world views Americans, one is obliged to mention the Middle East issue. No other issue comes close in demonstrating how different American perceptions can be from those of the rest of the world. This is the one issue in which the rest of the world expects America to rise up to its claim to be an extraordinary country providing moral leadership to the world.

To be fair, America has often done so: from the Camp David talks hosted by President Carter for Anwar Sadat and Menachem Begin to the enormous efforts made by President Bill Clinton just before he left office, America has done more than any other country to find peace in the Middle East. When it has failed, it has often been due to the failure of the parties. Yasser Arafat was strongly advised by the late King Hassan of Morocco to sign the peace offer worked out by President Clinton in late 2000. Regrettably, he failed to seize the opportunity, proving the wisdom of Abba Eban's famous quip that the Palestinians never miss an opportunity to miss an opportunity.

Unfortunately, the cost of these missed opportunities is paid not just by the people of Israel and Palestine (both of whom deserve their suffering to end soon) but also by the world as a whole. The Palestinian issue has unusual resonance among the 1.2 billion Muslims of the world, who feel humiliated by their inability to help their Palestinian brothers and sisters who are in obvious distress. No government of a predominantly Islamic country, not even one that is secular or modern, can afford to be seen to be less than totally supportive of Palestine. Neither can any American politician be seen to be less than totally supportive of Israel.

There is a clear and obvious political gridlock on the Middle East issue. Extraordinary efforts will be required to break the gridlock. Virtually the whole world supports the two-state solution put forward by President George W. Bush and the Road Map worked out by the Quartet (the U.N. Secretary-General, America, Russia, and the European Union). The tragedy here is that there is now almost a complete consensus among all key policymakers about what a final solution to the Middle East would be like: It would be similar to the Taba Accords worked out in January 2001 or to the virtual peace plan worked out by Yossi Beilin and Yasir Abed Rabbo in Geneva on October 12, 2003. In short, the directions for peace have never been clearer; the will to get there has never been more lacking. All claims by America to be an extraordinary country providing moral and political leadership to the world will ring hollow until some kind of peace is found in the Middle East. This will always be the litmus test for America's claim to leadership.

The one region of the world, however, that experienced the most pain and anguish from America's decision to become a normal country was the continent of Africa. Africa's problems are enormous. America did not cause them. But during the Cold War, America did intervene forcefully in Africa, propping up various governments that would not have survived without American support. When this support was withdrawn, several governments fell like a house of cards, like the government of President Mobutu of Zaire. Till today, Zaire (now called the Democratic Republic of Congo) has not fully recovered.

It is clear that America only wants to help Africa, not harm it. If it could, America believes that it would do nothing but help Africa. But what most Americans are unaware of is the extraordinary power differential between Africa and America. The vast majority of African countries are enormously weak. Often, American inaction in crucial issues can do enormous damage to these countries. Nothing illustrates this better than the tragic case of the genocide in Rwanda.

Eight hundred thousand Rwandans were killed between April and June 1994, many not with sophisticated weapons but with machetes. It was an episode that would haunt the United States and the United Nations: both President Clinton and U.N. Secretary-General Kofi Annan apologized publicly for their inaction. Rwanda proved to be a graphic illustration of the adverse effects of American power on the lives of people half a world away.

A few months before the genocide occurred, reports had begun to filter into the U.N. Headquarters from the U.N. field offices in Rwanda that preparations were being made for mass killings. These reports were fed to the U.N. Security Council, which has a responsibility to intervene to prevent genocide. But Rwanda was not of major interest or concern to any of the major powers, including America. The Security Council decided to ignore the reports from the field officers. Once the killings began, the Security Council was quickly and clearly told that the slaughter was genocidal. Some delegations pressed for the Security Council to condemn the "genocide" that was taking place in Rwanda. Any such condemnation would have obliged the Security Council to send in forces to halt the genocide. The American delegation to the Security Council therefore sought instructions from Washington on what to do.

Washington sent a clear response. The American delegation was instructed not to allow the use of the word "genocide" in any Security Council resolution. The reason was simple. America was a party to the Genocide Convention. If the Security Council had declared that a "genocide" was taking place in Rwanda, America (and other member states that had signed the convention) would have had a legal obligation to act and prevent the genocide. Since America wanted to avoid any legal obligation, it used its considerable influence to prevent the Security Council from condemning the genocide in Rwanda. In so doing, it not only prevented itself from halting the genocide in Rwanda, it also prevented the international community from doing so. Such is the extent of American power. When America decides that a nation should not be rescued, the international safety net is pulled away. And the distressed nations are abandoned to the great suffering of their peoples.

In May 2001, I visited the Great Lakes region in Africa as part of a U.N. Security Council mission. During this trip, we also visited Rwanda and Burundi, which have similar sets of ethnic tensions. While Rwanda had experienced genocide in 1994, Burundi has not. But Burundi remains fragile, with the danger of an ethnic conflagration remaining as real as ever. When our chartered plane landed in the capital, Bujumbura, one morning, the pilot made an announcement. He made an earnest appeal to all of us to finish our work and return to the plane before sunset. He told us that we had to fly out of the Bujumbura airport before sunset because after dark the rebels moved in closer to the city and would fire at planes taking off. This episode made us clearly aware how vulnerable Burundi was.

A few weeks later the Security Council ambassadors who had traveled to Burundi were invited to lunch with Gareth Evans, a former foreign minister of Australia who had become the head of the International Crisis Group, an NGO set up to monitor and advise on conflict situations around the globe. At the lunch, Evans turned to us and reminded us of our recent trip, and of how we had been made directly aware of the fragility of Burundi. He went on to ask us, if a similar genocide were to break out in Burundi as in Rwanda, what would the U.N. Security Council do this time? Intervene to prevent the genocide? Or again do nothing?

There was an awkward silence as the U.N. Security Council members pondered their response. After a while, an honest ambassador from one of the five permanent members of the Security Council (which are Britain, China, France, Russia, and the United States) raised his hand and said candidly, "My country has no vital national interest in Burundi. We will not intervene or lead an 'intervention.'" Soon every other major-country ambassador echoed his sentiment. The small-state representative knew that they could not intervene without the involvement of the major powers. There is no doubt that Gareth Evans was shocked by the response. He said, "Gentlemen, are you telling me that if a genocide breaks out in Burundi, the U.N. Security Council and the international community will again do nothing?" Silence greeted this comment.

Fortunately, Burundi has not suffered the same fate as Rwanda. As of 2004, no mass killings have taken place (although the conflict continues at a low simmer). Most citizens in key capitals, including most leading opinionmakers in major media organizations, believe that the international community has learned a lesson from the disastrous genocide in Rwanda in 1994 and they believe that it can never happen again. But as Gareth Evans learned in New York in 2001, nothing fundamental has changed. The "safety nets" set up to rescue nations in distress operate only when the interests of major countries are affected. And America is by far the most "major" nation of the world. The interests of America, not the conscience of America, will often determine whether lives will be saved or lost in many corners of the world.

Rwanda and Burundi are two of the poorest societies on the globe. It is difficult to understand why their ethnic rivalries have become so vicious. They were also unfortunate that they were colonized by Belgium, as the Belgian record as colonial rulers is among the worst. America should bear no responsibility for all this. But the problems of Rwanda and Burundi erupted at a time of American global dominance. American decisions were key in determining the outcomes of these tragedies.

It would certainly be unfair to place moral responsibility on America for all the ills of the world. The rest of mankind cannot evade its own responsibilities for its mistakes. Everything has to be kept in perspective. The purpose of the tragic tales I have recounted is not to try to assign blame on America. The purpose instead is to convey an even bigger message to an American audience that something really important happened in the 1990s. Wittingly or unwittingly, when the decade opened with the end of the Cold War, the world expected America to provide clear moral leadership to tackle these great crises, each of which brought grief to millions. These expectations may have been unfair, perhaps even unwarranted. But these expectations existed in the minds of billions. It was against these expectations that America was judged. And it was against these expectations that America was found wanting.

Perhaps a simple way of explaining these global expectations of America would be to begin by imagining what the rest of the world would have expected of the Soviet Union if (heaven forbid) it had "won" the Cold War instead of America. America would not have been destroyed. It would have remained a major power, exerting significant influence on its neighbors. But the global dynamic would not have revolved around America. It would have revolved around the Soviet Union. The world would have expected little from Moscow. For all the communist ideals espoused by the Soviet Union, the world knew that the Soviet Union was nothing more than a brutal power intent on promoting and protecting its national interests, not on advancing the interests of mankind. Certainly a Soviet leader could have also given a speech in which he or she spoke of giving weight to "opinions and energies of every person in the world." But any such speech would have rung hollow. The world could not conceive of the Soviet Union deciding to sacrifice or even align its interests to help the rest of mankind. But when America made such proclamations, as it often did, the world did not disbelieve them. These proclamations appeared to be consistent with American history and American values. Hence, not surprisingly, the world expected a lot more of America.

The world expected benign or moral leadership from America. Instead, as the decade of the 1990s unfolded, the world began to be aware that America was perhaps an ordinary country. The problem here was that this ordinary country had become massively powerful. Globalization had shrunk the physical and psychological space of our world. The rest of the world discovered that it was sharing this shrinking space with a large elephant. This large elephant did not intend to harm the other occupants. But it was nonetheless quite indifferent to the impact of its actions on the rest of the world. Gradually, as this became the perception of America around the world, the process of disillusionment began to grow.

No analogy can work perfectly to capture the complex relationship between America and the world. Still, if any kind of objective audit is made of key decisions made by America in the 1990s, one can list several actions that were taken in ostensible defense of American interests without much weight given to the impact of these actions on the rest of the world. Apart from the specific stories told in this chapter, there were other equally important decisions, like the decision to walk away from the Kyoto Protocol and the decision not to solve the problem of unpaid American dues to the United Nations. American unilateralism in the multilateral arena may have accelerated when the Bush administration came into office in January 2001. But it did not begin then. It had begun much earlier, when the end of the constraints of the Cold War allowed America to choose unilateral courses without worrying about any cost to American interests.

Ziauddin Sardar and Merryl Wyn Davies have also discussed the gap in understanding between Americans and non-Americans on the impact of American power:

> Most Americans are simply not aware of the impact of their culture and their government's policies on the rest of the world. But, more important, a vast majority simply do not believe that America has done, or can do, anything wrong. A poll of world "opinion leaders" in politics, media, business, culture and government, commissioned by the Paris-based *International Herald Tribune*, revealed that a majority of non-U.S. respondents—58%—felt that Washington's policies were a "major cause" in fuelling resentment and anger against the United States. In contrast, only 18% of U.S. respondents blamed their government's policies. Moreover, 90% of Americans listed their country's power and wealth as the chief reason why they are disliked, while the non-Americans overwhelmingly thought that the U.S. bears responsibility for the gap between the world's rich and poor. The poll suggested that "much of the world views the attacks as a symptom of increasingly bitter polarization between haves and have-nots"; and that America is largely responsible for developing countries "missing out on the spoils of economic progress."[9]

Time lags are inherent in international affairs. It takes time for the international community to fully absorb the significance of a new pattern of behavior. But this perception of American indifference to the rest of the world had begun to grow significantly over the course of the decade. The world began to judge America more rationally and objectively. The paradox here is that many of these new judgments of America were made by American-trained minds who had learned American social-sciences techniques to observe and understand new political and economic realities. Using the tools of American social science, they began to understand how America actually behaved towards the rest of the world. It then became obvious that the gap between American words and deeds had grown significantly in the course of the decade.

American scholars who are trying to understand the roots of anti-Americanism should therefore look at the record of American behavior in the 1990s as much as they look at the record of the second Bush administration in trying to understand the growth of these phenomena. Perceptions of people do not change overnight. They take time to grow and mature. Hence the change in sentiments towards America only began to emerge gradually.

I had noticed this change in perception as I traveled around the world and began speaking to different audiences. But despite picking up signals towards the end of the 1990s that perceptions of America had turned negative, I was still unprepared for the reactions of the world to the events of 9/11.

Most Americans are aware that there was a huge outpouring of public sympathy towards America when 9/11 occurred. This public sentiment of sympathy was best captured in the famous *Le Monde* headline which declared "Nous sommes tous Americains" (We are all Americans). There is no doubt that much of the public outpouring of sympathy was genuine. I was in Manhattan when 9/11 happened. I shared the shock and grief and my heart went out to the victims. All of us who lived in Manhattan, American or non-American, felt that we were part of the same human community in the face of this tragedy.

Three years have passed since 9/11 occurred. I have spoken to many of my friends all over the world about the day's events. Each remembers vividly where he or she was when the events occurred. It was a defining moment of world history. Billions of pairs of eyes watched the events unfold in front of their eyes as they watched the planes crash into the towers. For virtually every person I spoke to, the day's events, including what they did or heard on that day, have been indelibly etched onto their memories.

After hearing several of such first-person descriptions, I became aware that there were two strains in the reaction of the rest of the world to 9/11. There was the obvious and manifest public strain of sympathy for America and for the victims. But gradually, I began to be aware that there was an important private strain of reactions. The private reaction was less sympathetic. Among the unsympathetic private reactions there was a range of views, but the underlying theme in these reactions was the feeling that perhaps America deserved the attack for being so indifferent to the pain and sorrows of the rest of the world. Some people actually said that to me.

Over time, I began to hear even more disturbing stories of how some crowds who had watched 9/11 unfold on their TV sets had actually cheered when the two towers fell. Tom Friedman mentioned in one of his columns the story of American-trained doctors and nurses in Saudi Arabia cheering the collapse. I thought that this had to be an isolated incident. Since then I have heard similar stories from elsewhere. What was striking was that this had happened in both Islamic and non-Islamic societies. After checking again, I now have first-hand evidence that many of these stories are true.

These stories are one reason why I decided to write this book: to try to explain to an American audience why their perception of how they are viewed by the world has become so out of sync with how the rest of the world actually views Americans. Something has gone wrong somewhere. The good news is that many of these problems are not beyond solution. But to work out the solution, Americans first have to begin to understand the nature and depth of the problem they face. In some areas, especially in the Islamic world, the problem has become very serious.

Since 9/11, Osama bin Laden has become one of the best-known men on our planet. Through his deeds, he has proved that he is an evil terrorist. Americans have every reason to hate him with a vengeance. They probably expect the rest of the world to do so. Sadly, and this may be a commentary on the state of the world, the perceptions of Osama bin Laden in the rest of the world are mixed. Many fear and hate him. But many also secretly admire him, viewing him as a contemporary Robin Hood who had the skill and the guts to stand up to a big bad giant. As recently as February 11, 2004, at a football match in Guadalajara between the United States and Mexico, the Mexican crowd taunted the American football team with shouts of "Osama, Osama." The Mexicans could not find a better symbol to express their feelings towards America. In the Islamic world, the situation is more grave. I have done countless informal surveys, especially among my moderate Muslim friends, to find out who is the single most admired individual in the Islamic world. Without fail, only one name comes up: Osama bin Laden. Few Muslims support his terrorist activities; most admire him only for his ability to punch America in the face. He did something that many wish that they could have also done, if not as violently as he did.

~ 3 ~

America and Islam

*I*SLAM IS THE MOST SUCCESSFUL RELIGION in the contemporary world.

American perceptions of Islam are filtered by several layers of knowledge. At the root is the European understanding that has flowed into American consciousness as a result of the traditional Judaeo-Christian and European civilizational roots of most Americans. Most Americans celebrate the fact that America as a society represents in some ways the apex of Western civilization. It does. But the historical roots of Western civilization are deeply intertwined through centuries of contacts with the Islamic world. Many of the associations that have lodged in Western consciousness have not been happy ones.

The roots of Christian obsession with the Islamic world can be traced at least to the Crusades, if not earlier. It was at the Battle of Tours in 732 A.D. that Charles "The Hammer" Martel and the Franks turned the tide of Muslim expansion. Many heroic legends were created in the Crusades, launched at the end of the eleventh century. All of them had to do with heroic Christian knights battling perfidious Islamic "Saracens." Hence, for the Europeans, the word "Crusade" has always had a positive aura around it. Any man or woman who is fighting for a just or worthy cause can be said to be "crusading" for it.

Europeans are aware of the expansion of Islam into Europe. The conquest of Spain beginning in 711 A.D. is etched into historical memory as surely as the image of the Alhambra Palace dominates Granada. So too are all the maximal lines of the Islamic military invasion into Europe, culminating in the Ottoman Turks' siege of Vienna in 1683. Most Europeans believe that they narrowly avoided a cultural disaster when the Muslims marched into Europe. In their view, if Islam had triumphed in Europe as successfully as it had in other parts of the world (and Islam is still the most rapidly expanding religion of the world), it would have snuffed out the "lights" in Europe. Europeans believed that they came close to being wiped out by forces of darkness. This is the reason why Islam affects Western minds so strongly. There are deep, latent, historical fears buried in there. Five continuous centuries of Western triumph have not wiped them out.

It is equally significant that the enormous role played by the Islamic caliphates (in their moment of triumph and glory) of preserving the rich fruits of Greek and Roman civilizations (which still provide the spiritual and intellectual foundations of Western civilization) and then passing it back to Europe has not fully registered in the Western mind. Some Western intellectuals recognize the important role played by the caliphates. Chris Patten is one of them. As he said, "And what of Thomas Aquinas? He read Latin versions of the Greek philosophers, courtesy of the scholars at the Muslim School of Translation in Toledo, to which we owe so much of our knowledge of the scientific, religious and philosophical works of the ancient world."[1] Another is Daniel Rose, a New York philanthropist, who has advised that a rediscovery of Islam's glorious past could do good both for the West and for Islam. He said that we should reconnect the Arab world with "the Golden Age of the Abbassid Caliphate, when Muslim scientists, philosophers, artists and educators sparkled in one of the great cultural flowerings of all time." Rose added:

> Then Muslims remembered that the Prophet said 'The ink of scientists is equal to the blood of martyrs'; then Muslim thinkers were proud of their familiarity with the best of the world's cultures; then it was taken for granted that science and knowledge belonged to *all* mankind and that intellectuals' borrowing and lending benefited everyone. What the Muslims had once they can have again.[2]

Most ordinary Westerners are not aware of this rich history. Indeed if a survey is done of Americans, one in hundred, perhaps one in thousand, will be aware of the crucial role played by the caliphates in preserving the Graeco-Roman heritage for the West. What the West chooses to remember vividly and what it chooses not to remember reveals its attitudes. This is especially true of European attitudes towards the Islamic world. America, without knowing it, has inherited these historic European attitudes. (*Note*: This is one reason why I will speak interchangeably about "Western" and "American" attitudes towards Islam.)

There should in theory be no built-in tension between America and the Islamic world. Geopolitics often determines national policies. For most of its history America has never been threatened by the Islamic world. Most of the initial American contacts with the Arab and non-Arab Islamic worlds (and they have to be treated differently for analytical purposes) were benign. Indeed, after initial contacts, many deep and genuine friendships flourished between America and several Islamic societies, partly out of convergence of interests, partly out of the natural affection that flowed from intensive contacts. These friendships were real.

Several factors contributed. The American role in spurring European decolonization was recognized by Muslims worldwide. The distinction between prevailing American and European attitudes after World War II was brought out clearly during the Suez crisis of 1956 when Britain and France, working with Israel, made one last major attempt to regain the sphere of influence they had carved out in the region for over a century or more. To the region's surprise, America vetoed this move. The Arabs realized then that the Americans were different from European colonists. These positive Arab attitudes towards America in turn influenced the views of other Islamic communities, who have considered "Arabia" to be the center of the Islamic world.

The Cold War helped to deepen American relations with Islamic communities across the world. American policymakers began to realize that the Islamic world provided a natural buffer to the expansion of communism. There was a deep contradiction between the fundamental atheism of communism and the profound religiosity of Islam. The two could not coexist. Hence, even though there were occasional cynical realpolitik alliances between some states with predominantly Islamic populations (like Egypt under Nasser, Indonesia under Sukarno, Libya under Gadaffi) with the Soviet Union, communism could not seep one inch into Islamic soil. Neither Christianity nor Buddhism—the two religions with the next greatest numbers of adherents—provided fundamental obstacles to the expansion of communism. Islam did.

The peak of collaboration and cooperation between America and the Islamic world came after the Soviet invasion of Afghanistan in 1979. This invasion brought America and most of the Islamic world into a fairly firm alliance. American interests and the interests of Islamic states converged. When America destroyed the Soviet empire, it also woke up a sleeping dragon of Islamic sentiment. Afghanistan provided the first taste of victory to a group that had only experienced defeats for centuries. The victory of the mujahideen in Afghanistan may have provided to Islamic morale the same boost that the Japanese victory over Russia in 1905 had provided to other Asians. We know that one figure, Osama bin Laden, was inspired by the Soviet defeat in Afghanistan to believe that Islam could overwhelm a superpower.

When the Soviet empire crumbled and the Cold War came to an end, both America and Europe went dizzy with celebrations. Remarkable essays testifying to the indomitable spirit and strength of Western civilization were written. "The End of History" was one of them. The widespread applause it received showed a deep desire to believe that with the end of the Soviet empire, Western civilization had reached its apogee. "The End of History" suggested the rest of the world would soon learn that the best, and indeed only, way to progress was for all societies and civilizations to become in one way or another copies of the West. James Baker, then the American secretary of state, may have made a huge diplomatic faux pas when he spoke of the creation of a new community from Vancouver to Vladivostok (which clearly excluded Japan, an erstwhile powerful member of the Western club). But the spirit behind Baker's remarks was simple and clear: West is best.

Moments of great triumph produce moments of great blindness. As Western capitals were busy celebrating the triumph of the West, they failed to notice equally significant celebrations: the Islamic mujahideen warriors, who had come from all over the Islamic world to fight the Soviets in Afghanistan, believed that it was they who defeated the Soviet empire. They did not see any American or European warriors fighting by their side in Afghanistan. The mujahideen were happy to receive the Western weaponry but they also took note of Western "cowardice" about entering the battle-field directly. From this experience was born the powerful myth (which still emboldens the many supporters of Osama bin Laden) that the Islamic warrior will ultimately triumph over the Western warrior because the Islamic warrior is not afraid to die.

The tragedy here is that this victory has led to a perverted view among a small radical minority of Muslims. They believe that a life not spent in defense of the greatest faith, the Islamic faith, is a life wasted. Hence it is not surprising that suicide bombings have become a sunrise industry in all parts of the Islamic world: from Bali to Casablanca, from Riyadh to Istanbul. A new kind of warrior has emerged on the world stage: a warrior who will happily wrap explosives around his body and, on instructions, walk into any city and blow himself up. It seems sadly inevitable that it is only a matter of time before a Western city is struck by a suicide bomber. The warriors are ready. The opportunities will come.

There was nothing inevitable about this. It did not have to be this way. The religion of Islam is not inherently a religion of violence. "Islam" is often taken to mean "religion of peace." Islamic societies have lived in peace with themselves and in peace with their neighbors for centuries. Bernard Lewis is widely regarded as an authority on Islam. In one of his early essays, he wrote, "Islam is one of the world's great religions. Let me be explicit about what I, as a historian of Islam who is not a Muslim, mean by that. Islam has brought comfort and peace of mind to countless millions of men and women. It has given dignity and meaning to drab and impoverished lives. It has taught people of different races to live in brotherhood and people of different creeds to live side by side in reasonable tolerance. It inspired a great civilization in which others besides Muslims lived creative and useful lives and which, by its achievement, enriched the whole world."[3]

The militancy that we see growing in virtually every corner of the Islamic world is not a natural occurrence. It is a result of many factors, not the least of which is a series of flawed decisions that were made by Western policymakers in recent times. It takes a long time to accumulate reservoirs of hatred and anger. The West may not be aware of this but the current explosion of Islamist rage is the culmination of a century or more of Western action (and inaction).

I expect to be roundly attacked and criticized for suggesting that the West may indeed be partially responsible for many of the problems we see in the Islamic world. Hence, it may be useful for the reader to understand the credentials and background I bring to this subject. My mother, who passed away in 1998, would turn in her grave at the thought that her son could be perceived as a defender of the Islamic world. She could have easily been killed by a Muslim mob. Both my parents grew up as Hindu Sindhis in what is now Sind, Pakistan. The Hindus were an extremely small minority within the larger Muslim communities of Karachi and Hyderabad. From the time when Hindu-Muslim tensions emerged as part of the independence struggle, the Hindus lived in perpetual fear. There were riots and killings. My father's family was not spared. One of my uncles was killed as a very young man in a Hindu-Muslim clash in Karachi. When that happened, the Muslims who found the body brought it to my grandfather's house. Even though they had brought the body of his son to his house, my grandfather denied that it was his son. My grandfather feared that if he acknowledged that his son had been killed, the Muslim mob would kill him and all the rest of his family to ensure that no revenge was taken against them. Terror ran deep.

When partition came between India and Pakistan, all my Hindu relatives had to flee for fear of losing their lives in Muslim Pakistan. They gave up the land and businesses they owned and fled to all corners of the globe in 1947. I have first cousins in virtually every continent of the world, in North and South America, in Europe and Africa and all over Asia. It is a remarkable spread for one small family from a relatively tiny community, the Hindu Sindhi community. And wherever they went in the world, the Hindu Sindhis carried with them deep prejudices against Islam formed by these painful experiences. The Jews, in exile, always said, "Next year in Jerusalem." The Hindu Sindhis in exile have no hope of returning to Sind. Their homeland has been lost in perpetuity.

When my mother left Pakistan relatively late to join my father, who had already arrived in Singapore, she traveled by train through the desert from Pakistan to India. She was in the last car of the train with about forty to fifty other Hindu Sindhi women. They were protected by an old Sikh guard with a single-shot rifle. In the middle of the night, in the middle of the desert, the car they were in became decoupled from the rest of the train. They were stranded. In those days, when both Hindus and Muslims were killing each other with great abandon, there were marauding bands of young men on both sides who were looking for young women to rape and kill. The raping and killing of women of the other faith was seen as the ultimate humiliation to deliver to the other side.

The night that my mother spent in the decoupled train compartment was probably one of the most terrifying nights of her life. It scarred her for life. Fortunately, the next morning another train came along. The train's engine pushed my mother's decoupled car down the track until it reached a station in India. From there, my mother went to Singapore. It was my good fortune that my mother survived this harrowing experience. I was born a year later in Singapore in 1948.

Neither of my parents had the benefit of higher education. My father had six years of schooling, my mother ten. They naturally absorbed the prejudices they had grown up with. My mother, who was throughout her life a devout Hindu, had the stronger prejudice against the Muslims. When we were children, my mother's ultimate insult to anyone would be to say in Hindi, "wo toh musulman hai," meaning something like: "What else do you expect? He is Muslim, isn't he?" To be Muslim was to be perpetually condemned.

My mother arrived in Singapore and soon settled into a modest little row house. On both sides, we were separated from our neighbors by only a thin wall. We lived in 179 Onan Road. We and our neighbors at 177 and 181 Onan Road were constantly in and out of each other's homes. There were three children at 177, four children in our home at 179 and six children at 181. These thirteen children felt as though their three homes were one. The great irony here is that our home was devoutly Hindu. My neighbors were devoutly Muslim. At home, I was fed anti-Muslim prejudices. At play, I felt at home with the Muslims. Indeed, my family continues to maintain close friendly relations with these neighbors to this day.

These were Muslim Malays, not Muslim Arabs, Indians, or Pakistanis. Islam had arrived gently in Singapore, not through conquest but through traders who came from India. Conversion was gradual and consensual. Before the Muslim traders came, the Malays had a combination of Hindu and traditional beliefs. The Islam that spread to the Malay populations in Malaysia, Indonesia, and Brunei was easygoing. However, the Malays observed many of the requirements of the faith: fasting for a month in Ramadan, praying in the mosques, marrying in the faith.

They were good Muslims. But they and I also comfortably inhabited the world of English medium education in Singapore. The Malay Muslim schoolchildren wore Western clothes. Some young girls even wore mini skirts. In the late 1960s, we went to the discos together. Many young Muslims loved pop culture and sang Elvis Presley and the Beatles songs with great passion. There was no East-West divide between Islam and the West among the Malay Muslims in the 1960s.

Thirty years later, everything has changed. The young Malay Muslim girls I grew up with no longer wear Western dress. Most wear conservative Islamic dress, with only their face, hands, and feet showing. In the thirty years between the 1960s and 1990s, Islam underwent a significant transformation in Southeast Asia. The West did not seem even to notice.

Throughout the 1980s and 1990s, as globalization began to gallop ahead, the West was supremely confident that the enormous changes brought about by the forces of globalization and the shrinking of the world would deliver forces of modernization to all corners of the globe. The West did not take into account the fact that different parts of the world had different pools of history. Globalization facilitated the flow of a conservative brand of Islam through the world.

If the West had not shrunk the world through the forces of globalization it had unleashed, Southeast Asian Islam could have developed quite differently from the conservative forces of Arabic Islam. The conservative Arabization of Southeast Asian Islam was a direct result of Western technology. The West changed the face of Islam, but was unaware that it had done so.

A simple anecdote explains the nature of the change. In 1993, I was invited to the home of my then seven-year-old son's class teacher in Singapore. She was a young Muslim Malay woman who spoke English fluently and felt totally comfortable in a Western environment. But she dressed conservatively. Her husband was a middle manager in a shipping firm. They had a lovely five-room apartment. From all appearances, they were a typical successful middle-class family with dreams of doing better as the world progressed. One would think that they would have been happy with the state of the world.

But they were not. I spent an hour talking to her husband. There were only two issues that concerned him: Palestine and Bosnia. Through CNN and BBC, he had come to see scenes of Palestinians and Bosnians being killed. He described to me in great detail the many historical injustices inflicted upon the Palestinian and Bosnian peoples. A discussion about Palestine and Bosnia may seem natural to any highly educated middle class family in America or Europe. So what's the big deal about the discussion in a Malay Muslim living room in Singapore?

At that time, such a discussion in Singapore would have been as natural as a middle-class American family discussing the travails of the Christian Armenians in their struggle against the Muslim Turks and Azeris. Despite their common Christian heritage, the suffering of Armenians has not become common knowledge to Americans. In recent times, Christianity has not pulled Christians together to work for a common cause. But Islam has. The sufferings of Palestinians and Bosnians, who were virtually absent from Malay Muslim consciousness a few decades ago, have become deeply embedded in the Malay Muslim mind, thanks to Western technology.

All this was accomplished before the era of Al-Jazeera and the Internet. Now the vivid scenes of the sufferings of Palestinians, Iraqis, and Afghans under "foreign" occupation are broadcast even more frequently and vividly into Malay Muslim living rooms. The great irony here is that Al-Jazeera is also a Western creation. Before its arrival, the West lamented the lack of free independent TV stations in the Arab world. It celebrated the birth of Al-Jazeera. And the Al-Jazeera effect may well turn out to be one of the most important forces in creating a real sense of solidarity among the 1.2 billion Muslims who once lived in relatively distinct and separate communities. Al-Jazeera is now broadcast in Malaysia and Indonesia with Malay voiceover.

The decision to encourage the establishment of Al-Jazeera may be akin to that of a man throwing a match into a room where gasoline had been spilled. But this same man had also personally spilled the gasoline in the room. What was even more strange is that this man had earlier also attached his own house to this gasoline filled room before lighting the match. That, in one paragraph, summarizes recent Western policies towards the Islamic world.

Muslims have to bear the responsibility for most problems that bedevil their societies. In my first book, *Can Asians Think?*, I wanted to confront Asians with their lost thousand years of intellectual and economic development. If I were Muslim, I would have written a book, *Can Muslims Think?* (although I should add here that there is the tradition of the "gates of ijtihad" or independent reasoning in Islamic culture). But I am not a Muslim, so I cannot. Many Muslims want their societies to be as open and as successful as Western societies. Perhaps most still admire America and still want to emulate the best features of American society. It is in the interest of the entire world, including and perhaps especially America, that these moderate Muslims succeed.

One of the most perceptive and eloquent moderate Muslim voices I have encountered is that of an American citizen, Mahboob Mahmood. He now lives in Singapore but he has lived far longer in Manhattan than anywhere else. He has graduated from three of the United States's leading universities and has been a partner in a prominent American law firm. He was born a Pakistani, lived in a dozen places in Pakistan (ranging from Karachi to the Khyber Pass) and personally experienced many of the troubled events in Pakistan's history.

Having lived the first half of his life in Pakistan and most of the second half in America, he brings a unique perception to understanding the growing divide between America and the Islamic world. Indeed, soon after 9/11, Mahboob wrote a moving and insightful essay entitled "Getting Radical Over Terrorism." It traveled widely over the Internet but was unfortunately never published. Pity. It contains many insights that Americans should reflect on.

Mahboob explained in clear and simple terms why radical Islamic organizations have become so popular and powerful in the Islamic world. He argued that in the Islamic states with weak or corrupt governments, "Anyone who can create stakes for people can gain enormous power. In many of the Islamic states, hundreds of militant Islamic organizations have successfully done this. You may not agree with the ideology of these organizations, but you cannot dispute their success. These organizations provide an ideology and worldview, a moral framework, educational opportunities (there are over 50,000 Madrasahs in Pakistan alone), assistance for the poor and ill and an alternative law and order system. A few days ago, a friend told me a story about how, recently, a cow was stolen from a villager in Pakistan. The villager went to the police but they were unable to help him despite his offer of a small bribe. He then went to the fundamentalist Mullah (congregation leader) of the local mosque. During his sermon at the following Friday prayers, the Mullah cajoled and threatened the congregation and, by the following Sunday, recovered the cow for the villager (for no fee)."

By contrast, he added that in the same states "the leaders are not accepted by the people as legitimate; the politicians and generals have more money in overseas bank accounts than in their homelands; anywhere from 30% to 70% of the economy is untaxed, undocumented and illegitimate; and the most of the land is owned by people who rarely visit and never till the soil. In this parallel world, if you want land, you engineer government grants or collude with the land registrar; if you want electricity, you bribe the utility employee; if you want a loan, you 'monetarily befriend' the officer from the government-controlled bank; if you want to harass or kidnap someone, you work with the police; if you want to educate your children, you pay exorbitant tuition fees or you send them to a Madrasah (religious school); if you are a woman, you pray you marry someone who will not beat you; and, if you want (and can afford) a decent life, you emigrate."

Mahboob's key argument is that the whole socioeconomic and political condition of many Islamic states has provided a fertile ground for radical Islam organizations to grow and thrive. Mahboob freely acknowledged that the Islamic world is a troubled place. He states: "The 'Islamic world' is not a unified, homogenous brotherhood—it is at war with itself. As in the case of Europe during extended periods of her history, the 'Islamic world' has been convulsed in a prolonged period of instability and strife. Over the past thirty years, the internecine struggles between Muslim groups and states have claimed many more lives than the struggles between Muslim and non-Muslim groups and states. The massacres leading to Bangladesh, the Iranian revolution, the Iran-Iraq war, the Iraqi invasion of Kuwait, the weekly killings among Sunni and Shia groups in Pakistan, the black September killings in Jordan, the suppression by Turkey of the Kurds, the struggles between the Taleban and the Northern Alliance and the killings in Algeria are instances of bloodlettings within the 'Islamic world'."

Mahboob then added that "most of these conflicts have roots in the general failure of the leaderships of these countries to build legitimate and productive socio-political systems. Most of these conflicts also have roots in imperialistic European interventions and withdrawals that resulted in poorly drawn boundaries, shattered political orders and, in the case of Israel, the creation of a state through a process of colonization."

I have quoted the voice of a moderate American Muslim to demonstrate that many Muslims are aware of the troubled condition of the Islamic world. They have no illusion about the difficulties of modernizing the Islamic world. The natural assumption that any reader of this volume will have is that the West, including America, must have been helping the moderate Muslims.

The tragedy here is that the exact opposite has happened. Short-term interests have prevailed over long-term strategy. There is no coherent long-term Western or American plan to help the Islamic world. Instead the many confusing and conflicting strands of Western and American policies continue to destabilize the Islamic world. We will spend the most part of the twenty-first century handling the many problems generated by these confusing and conflicting policies.

The first strategic mistake made by the West was to assume that long-term interests were best served by a world in which Islamic states were mired in poverty and backwardness. The second strategic mistake, which flowed from the first, was a policy (never articulated, perhaps never conscious but nevertheless very real) *not* to share the successful policies of modernization with the Islamic world. The United States had a Marshall Plan to develop Europe after World War II, even a plan to develop Japan. The obvious question is why no such grand plan was devised for the Islamic world, or even for a few Islamic societies. Was it a result of pure ignorance of the need for one or of a calculation that the Islamic world was better off non-modernized? Historians will probably debate this for centuries. I have no doubt that Western and Islamic historians will reach opposite conclusions.

A third strategic mistake was to not see the huge importance of encouraging the success of Muslim moderates in Islamic societies. Many bright Western-educated Muslim minds are troubled by the poverty and backwardness of the Islamic world. They do not subscribe to the radical agenda of Osama bin Laden. Many of these Muslim moderates want their societies to be economically and politically compatible with the West, while remaining in social and spiritual terms true to their Islamic heritage. In short, they want to trigger both the equivalent of a renaissance and a rationalist enlightened movement in the Islamic world. They would make ideal partners of the West. But the West has not helped them. Instead the West has in recent decades helped those who suppress them.

The fourth strategic mistake of the West was not to consciously promote the spread of modern secular education in Islamic societies. Instead the West looked away or even quietly winked approval when $300 million per year of private Saudi money went into establishing wahabi-influenced Madrasahs, which fostered medieval fundamentalism, not modernity. These Madrasahs, quietly established in states that had supported the West in the Cold War, like Pakistan and Indonesia, have provided a ready pool of recruits for Osama bin Laden and Al-Qaeda and its affiliates. It takes an enormous effort to take a mind already steeped in ten years of wahabi education and re-educate it in the ways of the Modern world.

Mansour Al-Nogaidan, a journalist working for Al-Riyadh in Saudi Arabia, described in the *New York Times* his own long journey back from religious extremism: "For 11 years, from the age of 16, I was a Wahhabi extremist. With like-minded companions I set fire to video stores selling Western movies and even burned down a charitable society for widows and orphans in our village because we were convinced it would lead to the liberation of women. Then, during my second two-year stint in jail, my sister brought me books, and alone in my cell I was introduced to liberal Muslim philosophers. It was with wrenching disbelief that I came to realize that Islam was not only Wahhabism, and that other forms preached love and tolerance. To rid myself of the pain of that discovery I started writing against Wahhabism, achieving some peace and atonement for my past ignorance and violence." But few Muslims will be prepared readily to experience the "wrenching disbelief" necessary for them to revert from fundamentalism.

Husain Haqqani, a Pakistani columnist and a visiting scholar at the Carnegie Endowment for International Peace, has described his own experience in a Madrasah in Pakistan as a thirteen- year-old boy.[4] His teacher was a kindly old man, Hafiz Gul-Mohamed. Hafiz was angry with Husain only once, when Husain arrived for his lessons in his English school uniform instead of the traditional Islamic robes. Hafiz told Husain: "Today you have dressed like a *farangi* (European). Tomorrow you will start thinking and behaving like one. And that will be the beginning of your journey to hell."

Even so, Husain Haqqani added that the Madrasah he attended in the 1960s was relatively moderate. A few weeks after 9/11, Husain Haqqani visited the Madrasah in Pakistan that had taught the Taleban leader Mullah Omar. This Madrasah has been called "the University of Jihad". There, Husain met a nine-year-old boy, Mohamed Tahir, who explained his view of Islam: "The Muslim community of believers is the best in the eyes of God, and we must make it the same in the eyes of men by force. We must fight the unbelievers and that includes those who carry Muslim names but have adopted the ways of unbelievers. When I grow up, I intend to carry out jihad in every possible way."

Husain Haqqani has tried to explain why these Madrasahs have become so important in Pakistan and in the Islamic world: "The remarkable transformation and the global spread of madrasas during the 1980s and 1990s owes much to geopolitics, sectarian struggles, and technology, but the schools' influence and staying power derive from deep-rooted socioeconomic conditions that have so far proved resistant to change. Now, with the prospect of madrasas churning out tens of thousands of would-be militant graduates each year, calls for reform are growing. But anyone who hopes for change in the schools' curriculum, approach, or mind-set is likely to be disappointed. In some ways, madrasas are at the center of a civil war of ideas in the Islamic world. Westernized and usually affluent Muslims lack an interest in religious matters, but religious scholars, marginalized by modernization, seek to assert their own relevance by insisting on orthodoxy. A regular education costs money and is often inaccessible to the poor, but madrasas find it easy to believe that the West, loyal to uncaring and aloof leaders, is responsible for their misery and that Islam as practiced in its earliest form can deliver them."

After 9/11, America has joined other European societies in calling on countries like Pakistan and Indonesia to close down or change the education provided by these Madrasahs. But if these Madrasahs are the only source of education or social welfare in desperately poor areas, who will pay for the costs of developing an alternative that is equally fulfilling in both economic and spiritual terms? An American school cannot be parachuted into these areas to replace the Madrasahs. Instead, the school will have to be seen to be equally representative of Islamic values. This is why the suppression of Muslim moderates was such a catastrophic mistake.

The fifth strategic mistake made by the West was to implement economic policies that brought short-term electoral benefits to the democratically elected leaders in Western societies at the expense of long-term damage to Islamic societies. Any number of examples prove the point. Take one. After 9/11, President Musharaff and his country Pakistan immediately became a key ally in the battle against Osama bin Laden and Al-Qaeda. Not long after 9/11, he came to Washington, D.C., to seal this strategic partnership and friendship. To survive politically at home against the Islamic extremist parties, Musharaff, like a good Western politician, had to deliver economic benefits. He sought only economic concessions from America: a bigger textile quota to get more jobs in Pakistan. America turned him down. The few voters of North Carolina who were textile workers were more important than the larger national interest of America in helping Musharaff survive politically.

Cotton subsidies are having an even worse effect on the people of several African countries: "In the period from 2001 to 2002, America's 25,000 cotton farmers received more in subsidies—some $3 billion—than the entire economic output of Burkina Faso, where two million people depend on cotton. Further, United States subsidies are concentrated on just 10 percent of its cotton farmers. Thus, the payments to about 2,500 relatively well-off farmers have the unintended but nevertheless real effect of impoverishing some 10 million rural poor people in West and Central Africa."[5] Islam is spreading rapidly in these regions.

It is vital to recognize that the mistakes have been made over recent centuries. They have accelerated in recent times with the rapid shrinkage of the world. If any realistic change is to take place, the deep roots of the problem must be recognized.

Take the case of the first two strategic mistakes I mention above: the failure to share the fruits of modernization with the Islamic world. Unlike America, Europe does not sit an ocean away from the Islamic world. A small sea, the Mediterranean, separates Europe from North Africa. Thousands of Africans, including North African Arabs, have begun crossing it illegally to get into Europe. Hence the current European paranoia about immigrants. But in all this hysteria there is little attempt by Europe to understand what it may have done to instigate this trickle, which will by the end of this century become a flood unless Europe decides to deliver the obvious solution: export a successful model of development to an Islamic country, better still, to a group of Islamic countries.

It would be virtually impossible to find documentary proof that Europe made a strategic decision not to share its success with the Islamic world. The decision may not even have been conscious. Many such decisions are the product of visceral reflexes of Europeans towards Islam. Nor can I prove that the Europeans watched with smug satisfaction as one Islamic society after another failed to modernize in either the nineteenth or twentieth centuries, long after Europe had begun its steep upward climb, with the smugness redoubling as their former Islamic colonies stumbled rather than move forward after decolonization. None of this was ever expressed. It would have been politically impolite to do so. But among policymakers a quiet consensus developed that Europe would be better off with a struggling and underdeveloped Islamic world, which they assumed would pose a lesser threat to Europe than a successful Islamic world. We now know that the opposite is true. But so far, why has there been no change in European strategy?

The clearest proof of this can be found in European policies towards Turkey, which has throughout the twentieth century held the promise of being the first Islamic country to modernize successfully. It may well yet succeed. But if it does, it will not be as a result of any European assistance. Europe is at best ambivalent about Turkey. The powerful Ottoman Empire threatened Europe until 1918. Turkey's large population is growing much faster than Europe's. Already there are several million migrant Turkish workers in Europe, especially in Germany. Unlike in America, most migrant workers, especially Muslim migrant workers, do not integrate themselves well into European society. Europe is not a land of migrants. The natural inclination of Europe, from the very first days that Turkey expressed a desire to integrate itself into Europe, was to draw up the ramparts to keep Turkey out. Europe believed that the European Union would be more secure without Turkey. Actually, by keeping Turkey out, Europe has only planted the foundation for long-term insecurity. "Slamming the gates of Brussels would leave Turkey isolated and growling on the borders of Europe, its pro-western consensus in tatters and the darker forces of the Turkish right unleashed. Absorbing Turkey, maybe in a decade's time, will be an enormous challenge, but not nearly as enormous as the risk of cutting it adrift."[6]

Turkey has for several decades applied to join the European Union (EU). The European Union has never formally said 'No.' Instead it has declared, with some validity, that Turkey has not met many of the conditions for joining: Turkey's human rights record has flaws. Turkey allowed the death penalty. Turkey had occupied part of Cyprus. But in their heart of hearts, the Europeans knew that these were only excuses. Even if Turkey had met all the conditions and even if it had had an exemplary human rights record, it would have been kept out of the EU for one simple reason: the Turks are Muslims. The Christian members of the EU did not feel comfortable sharing the common house of Europe with an Islamic member. Few European leaders would have the courage to admit this openly. But the former French President Giscard d'Estaing, who had been tasked in 2003 to draft a new constitution for Europe, declared publicly that Turkey could never be admitted into the European Union. His exact words were, "Its capital is not in Europe, 95 percent of its population live outside Europe: it is not a European country. . . . [Turkey has] a different culture, a different approach, a different way of life. . . . [If Turkey is allowed to join,] in my opinion, it would be the end of the European Union."

Giscard d'Estaing was only expressing publicly what many Europeans believe privately. They fear that by admitting Turkey they will be bringing an Islamic Trojan horse into Europe. The tragedy here is that few European policymakers, if any, saw that the admission of Turkey into the EU may well have had exactly the opposite effect: the smuggling of a secular Trojan horse into the Islamic World.

Turkey is already a secular country. In fact, many Turkish citizens met the election of Prime Minister Recep Tayyip Erdogan with shock because Erdogan was a devout Muslim. The Turkish public's worries about a devout Muslim at the head of their secular government were not echoed by President Bush, however, who said, "You believe in the Almighty, and I believe in the Almighty. That's why we'll be great partners."[7] Frankly, that sentiment needs to be more widely shared. Leaders who are members of different faiths, like those of Europe and Turkey, need to recognize the vast potential for growth to be had through cooperation across the religious gap.

The extremists who bombed the two synagogues in Istanbul in November 2003 knew exactly what they were doing. Turkey has always wanted to be both a Western and Islamic country. One way it stood out from its neighbors in the Arab world was its willingness to both maintain relations with Israel and to allow the Jewish community in Turkey to continue. The Jews arrived in Turkey when they were expelled from Spain in 1492. They have lived in Turkey for 500 years. The Islamic extremists sought to damage Turkey's relations with Israel, thereby creating a breach between Turkey and the West. Fundamentalism thrives on separatism. The EU should counter it by embracing Turkey.

Instead, for the past few decades, European policymakers have been worrying about how to diplomatically decline Turkey's application to join the European Union. It is surprising that the Europeans have not paused to consider the alternative scenario: What if Turkey withdrew its application to join the EU and decided to no longer be a bridge between the West and Islam? Which other nation could offer to play this role? Fortunately, Turkey does remain a member of some Western clubs, including NATO and the Council of Europe. These help to mitigate the problem.

The fate that Turkey has faced in trying to build bridges between the West and the Islamic world is similar to the one faced by Muslim moderates as they try to build similar bridges on an individual level. Like the proverbial joke about the man who walks in the middle of the road and consequently gets hit by both sides, these individual Muslim intellectuals find it difficult to get a receptive audience in either the West or in the Islamic world.

After 9/11, many of these Muslim intellectuals wrote anguished pieces trying to understand the circumstances that had led to the tragic events of 9/11. They felt deeply angry and embarrassed over the obvious equation in the Western mind of the religion of Islam with massive acts of terrorism. This was a key result of 9/11. Moderate Muslim intellectuals wanted to convince the West that Islam was not about extremism. But they also wanted to explain the anger that many Muslims felt towards Americans and the West. This was one reason why Mahboob Mahmood wrote his essay after 9/11.

Over two years have passed since Mahboob Mahmood wrote his essay in an effort to wake up his fellow Americans on the need for a new set of American policies to handle the Islamic world. The reason why so little has changed is because America has allowed Osama bin Laden to dictate the terms of the engagement between Islam and America. Indeed, this has prompted Richard Holbrooke, a former U.S. ambassador to the United Nations, to ask, "How has one man in a cave managed to out-communicate the world's greatest communications society?"[8] Osama bin Laden wants only a military engagement. In this he has succeeded. Since 9/11, the United States has successfully invaded and occupied Afghanistan and Iraq. In both cases America has won spectacular battlefield victories that have confirmed for many the overwhelming military superiority of America.

But consider the possibility that Osama bin Laden may actually regard these American military invasions into Afghanistan and Iraq as a great victory for him instead. Osama bin Laden may have had two strategic goals when he launched his attacks on 9/11. His first goal was to make Americans feel pain directly. As he said in an interview, "Why should fear, killing, destruction . . . continue to be our lot, while security, stability and happiness be your lot? This is unfair. It's time we get even. The Islamic nation has started to attack you at the hands of its beloved sons. You will be killed just as you kill, and you will be bombed just as you bomb and expect more that will further distress you . . ."[9]

In being able to inflict pain directly onto the Americans, he also became a major heroic figure in the contemporary Islamic imagination, the only Islamic figure who could do something effective to alleviate the humiliation that most Muslims feel about their condition. Many Americans would like to ask these Muslims to be rational and realize that Osama bin Laden has no long-term answer to their economic problems. But just as Americans reacted viscerally when they were attacked, the Muslims also reacted viscerally to Osama bin Laden. They celebrated him because he punched the huge Goliath called America and got away with it. This is why when 9/11 happened, many Muslims around the world—including in Islamic communities friendly to America—rejoiced. Americans who are unaware of this simple but sad reality are either out of touch with the real world or in a state of denial about it.

Osama bin Laden's popularity remains strong two years after 9/11. A survey conducted by the Pew Research Center in February/March 2004 noted the enduring popularity of Osama bin Laden in Muslim countries, rated favorably by 55 percent of those surveyed in Jordan, 65 percent in Pakistan and 45 percent in Morocco. All these countries are key allies of America. In trying to explain this popularity, Andrew Kohut, the director of the Pew Center, said, "The Muslim publics come off feeling beleaguered in relation to the rest of the world. It's an in-your-face attitude and it reflects a real vein of discontent with us."[10]

Osama bin Laden's second strategic goal may have been to lure American military boots on to Islamic soil and create visual images of direct American/Islamic confrontation. Until 9/11 happened, there had been few American troops on the soil of Islamic countries. There had been a few American peacekeepers in Beirut in President Reagan's era. There were also American military bases in Saudi Arabia, a key source of irritation for Islamists, who cited a deathbed utterance of the Prophet Mohammad: "Let there not be two religions in the Hijaz" (that is, Mecca and Medina). Similarly there had been some American peacekeepers in Somalia (and their unfortunate decision to cut and run after eighteen American soldiers were killed in Somalia helped strengthen the myth that American society cannot tolerate military casualties). After 9/11, America overthrew two governments in Islamic countries. This will be a boon to fundamentalist preachers.

The mind of Osama bin Laden is obviously warped in many ways. But that does not preclude the possibility that he may have some shrewd Machiavellian instincts. Before 9/11, there had been anger accumulating against America in the Islamic world because of America's strong support of Israel. But the focus of the anger was Israel. America was seen only as the supporter, not the lead actor. Osama bin Laden wanted to send a simple and clear message to ordinary Muslims worldwide that the real enemy of Islam was not Israel but America. Osama bin Laden's former bodyguard told the London-based Arab newspaper, *Al-Quds Al-Arabi*, on August 3, 2004:

> The Al-Qa'ida organization's goal from its inception is to sow conflict between the United States and the Islamic world. I remember that Sheikh Osama bin Laden used to say that we can not, as an organisation, continue in quality operations (like 9/11), but rather we must aspire to commit operations that will drag the United States into a regional confrontation with the Islamic peoples.[11]

He may have achieved this with the military invasions of both Afghanistan and Iraq. He could have reasonably calculated that no matter how careful America was with these military invasions (and in both invasions the American military was extraordinarily careful in trying to avoid civilian casualties), mistakes would be made. Innocent civilians would be killed. Mosques would be destroyed. The forces of nationalism and Islamic anger would be naturally ignited. And Muslims all over the world would feel a sense of shame that two troubled societies in the Islamic world had to be put right by American interventions. Many sophisticated Muslims were aware that in both cases, American intentions were benign. America has no desire to occupy either Iraq or Afghanistan for a long period. Indeed the American people would be happier if those two societies could be quickly "fixed" and returned to their citizens, allowing American soldiers to return home quickly and safely. But no matter how benign the intentions, the American entry into both Afghanistan and Iraq has only reinforced the sense of humiliation that Muslims already feel.

Osama bin Laden, given his reportedly frail health, may not live much longer. But if he were to die now, he may well die a satisfied man. By his calculations, in any *in*direct competition between America and the Islamic world, there would be little he could do to harm America. But if he could get Americans directly engaged in confrontation on Islamic soil, the Islamic world would eventually triumph. Osama bin Laden believes history is on his side. First, Islam has been around for 1,400 years, America for only 230 years or so. Second, Islam generates a very high degree of devotion and adherence among its believers. Third, there are far more Muslims in the world than Americans, 1.2 billion compared to 290 million. These Muslims, unlike the 1.3 billion Chinese in China, are spread over a wide swath of the world. Hence, they could attack American interests in an area stretching from Casablanca to Bali. Fourth, thanks to the American export of the radical idea that every human being deserves to be treated with equal dignity and respect, the Islamic world has begun to be aware in the closing decades of the twentieth century that Islamic societies all over the world are relatively backward and hence downtrodden. There is a sense of ferment in the Islamic world about this relative backwardness. On this fertile soil, Osama bin Laden had planted the idea that Muslims can regain some of their dignity by fighting the Americans. So far

Osama bin Laden has been successful in tapping the ferment. A hundred years ago it would have been inconceivable for Moroccans and Javanese, Saudis and Filipino Muslims to believe that they were brothers bound together in a common struggle. Now it is not just conceivable. It has happened.

Thus one can begin to understand how different the perceptions are in America and in the Islamic world about their latest direct encounters in Iraq and Afghanistan. The same scenes can look very different through different eyes.

American policymakers see their interventions in both Afghanistan and Iraq as brief surgical incisions, limited in time and scope. America entered these two territories with specific objectives: to kill or capture certain individuals (Osama bin Laden, Mullah Omar, Saddam Hussein), remove the corrupt, authoritarian governments, and replace them with democratically elected, modernizing, pro-American governments that would benefit the Afghan and Iraqi people as they focused on development instead of the military adventures of the Taleban and Saddam Hussein. In so doing, America would win the battle against terrorism, and the hearts and minds of Islam. Both America and the world would become safer after American military successes. All this would be accomplished within the political constraints imposed by the need to deliver successes in every four-year political cycle. In short, limited goals, limited means, and carefully defined limited results.

The big challenge that America faces in fighting the global jihad of Al-Qaeda and its ilk is that it has to wage both a military and political campaign and both campaigns have to reinforce each other. Some senior officials in the Bush administration realize this. In a memo that he wrote to senior Pentagon officials on October 16, 2003, Defense Secretary Donald Rumsfeld said: "Are we capturing, killing or deterring and dissuading more terrorists every day than the madrasahs and the radical clerics are recruiting, training and deploying against us? Does the U.S. need to fashion a broad, integrated plan to stop the next generation of terrorists? The U.S. is putting relatively little effort into a long-range plan, but we are putting a great deal of effort into trying to stop terrorists. The cost-benefit ratio is against us! Our cost is billions against the terrorists' cost of millions."[12]

This memo by Donald Rumsfeld was in turn quoted in the comprehensive and thoughtful report put out by the 9/11 Commission. The report emphasized that a strong military response, including preemptive strikes, was essential in the battle against terrorism, but this alone was not enough. As the report said, "The first phase of our post–9/11 efforts rightly included military action to topple the Taleban and pursue Al-Qaeda. This work continues. But long-term success demands the use of all elements of national power: diplomacy, intelligence, covert action, law enforcement, economic policy, foreign aid, public diplomacy and homeland security. If we favor one tool while neglecting others, we leave ourselves vulnerable and weaken our national effort."[13]

To be fair to the Bush administration, it has marshaled the extensive international networks that America has developed in the intelligence, military, and diplomatic fields and led a global response to this threat from Islamic terrorism. No one can doubt the resolve of the Bush administration in this battle. But despite this robust response, it is uncertain whether the jihadis terrorists have been intimidated.

Osama bin Laden and his supporters may have a different perspective on the American struggle against terrorism. In their view, instead of "draining the swamp," the arrival of American troops extended and deepened the quagmire. The farther in they marched, the deeper they sank. The Iraqi and Afghan identities had been shaped by centuries of history. So too their sense of Islam. Osama bin Laden and his friends saw innocent Americans wading unwittingly into these pools of history, and gradually, inevitably, getting lost. Mistakes were made. Afghan and Iraqi nationalism was reignited. Before long, America was trapped. The stronger the American military reaction, the stronger would be the Islamic political reaction. America wanted to get out of these two countries as quickly as possible; Osama bin Laden and his friends were content to watch America wallow. The longer America stayed, the more it would become intertwined with Islamic history. In the first decade, perhaps even in the first century, the forces of Islam might lose. But this was, in their eyes, a thousand-year battle. A thousand years ago, the Muslim world expelled the Christian crusaders. A thousand years from now the Muslims would triumph over the Americans.

Americans may be puzzled by this strong sense of millennial confidence shown by a religious group whose adherents live in societies so far behind America in development. The economic gap between America and Islamic societies is growing. So too is the American lead in science and technology. Hence, it would make sense for Americans to show absolute confidence that they will win this war. On what basis do some Muslims believe that they will eventually triumph over America?

It is because Islam is the most successful religion in the modern world. One of my three children, who was then studying in high school at a private school in New York City, happened to spot the first sentence of this chapter when I wrote it. She said to me, "I know what the sentence means. It means that Islam is growing faster than any other religion." I told her that that was only part of it.

The full implication of the sentence is evidenced in a Pew study concerning the importance of religion in different countries. The study found that America stood alone among wealthy nations in placing high value on religion. Fifty-nine percent of Americans "say that religion plays a *very* important role in their lives." Fewer than 15 percent of Japanese, French, and Russians said the same, as did fewer than 35 percent of British, Italians, Germans, and Koreans. In contrast, in Muslim countries like Pakistan and Indonesia, over 90 percent of the population considered religion very important. No African country out of the ten surveyed had a result of less than 80 percent. These numbers communicate an important message. Islam has no room for the type of religious believers that have grown in non-Islamic countries, the people who go to church once or twice per year on major holidays.

Islam both demands and receives more from its adherents. A Muslim is expected to pray five times a day. For many this is not practical. But for the mandatory Friday afternoon prayers there are massive turnouts in the mosques. During the fasting month of Ramadan, virtually all Muslims fast from sunrise to sunset. This can be very demanding, but a successful achievement of fasting during this month strengthens the believer's conviction in his Islamic faith. Islamic rituals are also an important part of each passage of life.

More importantly, there has been no secular revolution in the Islamic world. Turkey has gone furthest in separating church from state. But the trend even in Turkey is towards greater religiosity. As Turkey becomes more democratized under European and American pressures, Islamic parties are winning the elections. Bertrand Russell could write his fierce essay on "Why I am not a Christian" several decades ago and not face death or persecution in a Christian society. Almost no Muslim intellectual could write an equivalent essay and hope to get away with it (except perhaps in Turkey). The religious fatwa that was issued against Salman Rushdie for his writing *The Satanic Verses* sent a clear signal that apostasy could never be accepted in any part of the Islamic world. This is another reason for growing incomprehension between Islam and the West. In many Western countries, religion is steadily playing a diminishing role in political life. In Islam, its role is becoming more important.

The net result of all this is that Islam as a religion plays a far greater role in the life of its adherents than any other religion, be it Christianity, Hinduism, or Buddhism, all of which also have large pools of believers. Hence the teachings and sermons conveyed to the Muslims matter more than those conveyed to Christians, Hindus, or Buddhists. Yet if one were to try to scan the Western media for any record of either the contents or the trend lines in the messages of Islamic sermons and teachings, one would find virtually no comment or understanding of them. This ignorance is remarkable. More than one billion Muslims are having their attitudes to the world increasingly shaped by these sermons and teachings. Yet the world as a whole is not listening to the messages. Occasionally even more dangerous messages are propagated through music and folklore. In January 2004, a popular Egyptian singer, Sha'ban Abd Al-Rahim, released a song with the key line saying, "Hey People It was Only a Tower and I Swear by God that They [the U.S] are the Ones Who Pulled It Down." Abd Al-Rahim further sang that "they" purposely did it to make people think that Arabs and Muslims are terrorists and were behind that disaster. Now the United States could do what it pleases to the Arab world since everyone thinks Arabs were to blame.[14] A young friend of mine studying Middle Eastern Studies in Harvard alerted me to this song and added "an interesting piece on how Egyptian pop music (which is listened to across the Arab world) solidifies anti-Americanism—conversely, imagine Britney Spears or U2's Bono singing about the evils of Islam."

The Western media is only now taking its first baby steps into revealing Islamic culture to the average American. An article in the *New York Times* in September 2003 described the difference between Western and Islamic views on martyrdom. In the Middle East, the word *shahid* originally carried with it the same religious connotations as the English word *martyr*. These days, though, anyone killed in battle is a *shahid*, because in Islamic culture, war is inherently a matter of religion. "The widespread use of a religiously loaded word like *shahid* in popular Muslim culture is a hint of a mindset that also makes it almost inevitable that Muslims in the Middle East will see the West's actions in their region in religious terms. And it is subtle cultural gaps like these that make it harder for us to live peaceably in a world that gets ever smaller—unless we make an effort to understand one another."[15]

This is why America needs a massive wake-up call. It is walking into Islamic societies in a far greater way than it ever has in its or in Islamic history. Yet it is doing so with little understanding or comprehension of the powerful forces that it is both igniting and dealing with. If Osama bin Laden represents just another misguided individual—the sort that mankind has produced from time to time, like Hitler or Pol Pot—then the problem would automatically be solved with his elimination. But if his anger, thoughts, and visions (not his actions!) are the embodiment of a strong strand of beliefs in the minds of many others, than his elimination solves nothing. It is this strong strand of beliefs that has to be handled. Neither America nor the West has any comprehensive long-term policy to deal with it.

But all is not lost. A large number of moderate Muslims have studied in the West, Muslims like Mahboob Mahmood, whom I have quoted extensively in this chapter. Indeed when I finished writing the first draft of this chapter, I sent it to Mahboob for his comments. He said that he found the draft chapter (which has since been modified) "incisive and evocative" and he did not have any specific comments on the text. However, he kindly drafted a note which contained thoughts of his that he felt could dovetail with the end of my chapter. I am happy to publish his note as a postscript to this chapter. Here is the voice of Mahboob Mahmood:

> In the rest of this chapter, I will not try to lay out any such policy for America and the West. Instead, I will try to establish the

"ground zero" of any such policy—the realities such policy must confront and address.

In his seminal work, *The Selfish Gene,* Richard Dawkins introduces the notion of a 'meme'. In the same way that genes contain the DNA to replicate specific characteristics of living organisms, Dawkins argues that memes replicate patterns of human thought or behaviour: "Just as genes propagate themselves in the gene pool by leaping from body to body via sperms or eggs, so memes propagate themselves in the meme pool by leaping from brain to brain via a process which, in the broad sense, can be called imitation." A meme could include an idea (e.g., notions about the role of America in the world), a methodology (e.g., how to set up and fund a Madrassah or religious school) or a behaviour (e.g., becoming a suicide bomber). Just like genes, memes are enormously powerful because they are patterns of thinking and behaviour that are capable of infinite and unplanned replication—they do not need an explicit leader, text or centralized intervention.

In the Western world, patterns of thinking and behaviour (originally inspired by liberal and rationalist thinkers and leaders) relating to democratic government, civil liberties, freedom of speech, tolerance, methodologies to engage in economic activity, etc., have achieved the characteristics of a cluster of memes. Similarly, in the Islamic world, patterns of thinking and behaviour (originally inspired by fundamentalist and militant thinkers and leaders) relating to the role of religion in society, ideas about the sources of truth, hostile attitudes to the West, ideas about Jihad and self-sacrifice, methodologies to establish schools and raise money, etc., have achieved the characteristics of a cluster of memes.

This militant Islamic meme cluster no longer requires particular texts, thinkers, leaders or instructional guides. This meme cluster—and this is my first point regarding the "ground zero" of our present situation—is capable of being replicated (and is actually being rapidly replicated) throughout the Islamic world without the need for a centralized motive force. As an example, in Pakistan, the number of Madrasahs (religious schools) mushroomed from under 1,500 in 1980 to over 50,000 in 2000 without any kind of central planning or funding. [Note: These figures are estimates. No precise data are available.] Only thinking and behavior patterns that have become memes are capable of such phenomenal growth.

My second point is that a cluster of memes can only be overcome by another cluster of memes. The real battleground is, as it were, at the level of the DNA of culture—not at the phenomenal level of particular leaders (such as Osama bin Laden), particular groups (such as Al-Qaeda) or particular ideas (such as the militant idea of suicide bombings as a form of Jihad). It is not enough to militarily target a particular group (such as the Taleban), or to diplomatically contain a particular regime (such as the Iranian regime), or to systematically restructure the polity of a particular country (such as by introducing 'democracy' in Iraq). Unless and until the Islamic world internalizes and implements a countervailing cluster of memes, the militant Islamic meme cluster will only continue propagating. A good policy must engage at the level of the DNA of Islamic culture.

My third point is that the phenomenal propagation of the militant Islamic meme cluster within Islamic societies does not represent the ineluctable extension of their pasts into their futures. The Islamic meme cluster is displacing two weaker but nevertheless widely prevalent meme clusters—the traditional and the modern. Each Islamic society includes a rich variety of traditional clusters of thinking and behaving—expressed though tribal and clan structures, geographical ties, indigenous languages and local customs. Each Islamic society also includes liberalized, Western populations who yearn for tolerant, non-religious, rule-bound forms of social and political organization. Militant Islam has asserted itself against the weakening of the mimetic power of traditional society and the fledgling mimetic potential of modern society. A good policy can only grow out of a thorough understanding of, and a vision for positively leveraging, these tensions within Islamic societies.

My final point is that the Islamic meme cluster, like others, is likely to contain within it the seeds of its own destruction. Is militant Islam capable of delivering all it has promised? The central promise of militant Islam is creation of a just society. The importance of the notion of justice in Islamic societies cannot be over-emphasized—in these societies, freedom, democracy and rule of law are weak memes—but justice is a strong meme. The delivery of justice is and always has been the kernel of Islamic socio-political thought. Up to today, militant Islam has succeeded by emphasizing the injustice of the prevailing order—whether it is the treatment by the House of Saud of the Saudi population or the unevenness of U.S. policy in the Middle East. To the extent that the Islamic meme cluster represents the most just system for its participants, it will prevail and flourish. But to the extent countervailing traditional and modern approaches are able to deliver a greater degree of justice—in a form that can be propagated as a meme—then the power of militant Islam will begin to recede. A good policy will only succeed if it is capable of addressing and defeating militant Islam on the grounds of its central promise and its ultimate incapability—the creation of a just society.

~ 4 ~

America and China

MERICA'S RELATIONS with the 1.2 billion Muslims in the world are clearly in trouble. If America is not careful, its relations with 1.3 billion Chinese could be heading the same way. In strategic terms, it would be unwise for the 290 million Americans to have a difficult relationship simultaneously with two groups of people who, combined, have a population almost ten times that of America's. Their minds enveloped in the current mood of hubris, it is difficult for some key American thinkers to accept the suggestion that a little bit of prudence should be injected into American policies.

America has been imprudent in its policies towards China. It has used China when it suited American geopolitical interests and ditched it when it no longer served American interests. Since the end of the Cold War, as part of the post–Cold War hubris, America has presumed that a young nation just over two centuries old could remake a five-thousand-year-old civilization in its image. In the

1990s, China was beginning to enter into one of its most peaceful and prosperous periods, after more than a century of civil wars, foreign humiliations, internal convulsions, and wars at its doorstep. It was precisely at the moment when the Chinese felt that they were standing up with dignity that America noisily discovered that China's human rights record was blemished. Hence America decided to portray China as an unfortunate relic of the Soviet Communist era, one that would be washed away by the new tide of freedom and democracy spilling all over the world. At dinner parties, thoughtful Americans could only ask: "How long will this Chinese Communist regime last?" When thoughtful Chinese met, the main question they asked was, "How long can we prolong this wonderful period of peace and prosperity we are finally enjoying?" When those thoughtful Americans saw the Chinese government on the verge of extinction, the Chinese saw themselves as finally having surfed the tide of history that would restore China to its rightful place in the first league of nations.

How could America have so misunderstood China? It was not for lack of information. There is no shortage of China scholars in America. How could the best and freest media in the world not get the "big story" right? The sharp competition in the marketplace of ideas in America is supposed to ensure that the "truth" will eventually surface and distortions disappear. But this belief too contributes to the current perception of American hubris.

One simple story illustrates how two peoples can see reality in exactly opposite ways. On May 7, 1999, American missiles struck the Chinese embassy in Belgrade. Three Chinese were killed. This was seen by the Western and American media as just one small incident, unfortunate though it may have been, in the painful war in the Balkans. It was reported for a day or two, then largely forgotten.

Those American foreign policy devotees who recall the attack are convinced that it was an accidental bombing by an American aircraft. Asked if it was deliberate, 99 percent would say that any such claim was preposterous and absurd.

Most Chinese have *not* forgotten this event. Virtually all Chinese I have spoken to are convinced that the American bombing of the Chinese embassy was deliberate. They point out that American surveillance technology is so sophisticated that it can pick out a moving car from a satellite. How could sophisticated American surveillance not have known the position of the Chinese embassy? Many also believe that the attack's purpose was to send a message to China: Beware of American power.

In our current era of growing transparency, with so much information available on virtually every major international event, how could one single event be interpreted so differently by two peoples? The simple answer is that there is a huge divide in the way Americans and Chinese see the world. Americans like to believe that there is only one right way. But their perception is not necessarily shared by others.

America and China could well have been heading on a collision course as the twenty-first century opened. In April 2001, an American spy plane crash-landed on the Chinese island of Hainan after a mid-air collision with a Chinese jet fighter not far from Chinese shores. The pilot of the Chinese jet fighter, Wang Wei, perished. All the American crew survived. The Chinese government detained the American crew for eleven days. During this period, there were both diplomatic overtures and belligerent noises from America as it demanded the immediate safe return of the crew and the plane. Eventually the crew members were released. The episode seemed to be a sign that American and Chinese relations were on the brink.

It was widely believed then that the prevailing superpower of the day would not allow the emergence of a potential competitor. Of course, this was never the explicit policy of the American government. But many of the key policymakers in the Bush administration in early 2001 had come together ten years earlier and produced a document entitled "Defense Planning Guidance." One of the key elements in the document was a declaration that America should do all in its power to prevent the emergence of a competitor. Its exact words were, "Our first objective is to prevent the re-emergence of a new rival. This is a dominant consideration underlying the new regional defense strategy and requires that we endeavor to prevent any hostile power from dominating a region whose resources would, under consolidated control, be sufficient to generate global power. These regions include Western Europe, East Asia, the territory of the former Soviet Union, and Southwest Asia."

Anyone assessing the likely immediate future for Chinese-American relations in April 2001 would have produced a very gloomy forecast indeed.

Five months later, 9/11 happened. 9/11 may have saved China. Before then, when American strategic thinkers focused on potential threats, they only saw China. After 9/11, America has focused on the threat posed by Osama bin Laden, Al-Qaeda, and similar terrorist groups emerging from the Islamic World. China shrewdly calculated that it could use this moment to demonstrate its strategic usefulness to America.

This unexpected consequence of 9/11 raises a fundamental question: Can the relationship between the world's greatest power and the world's greatest emerging power be left purely to be determined by chance events? Or should there be a long-term strategy? The answer should be obvious. To avoid major crises in the twenty-first century, it would be wiser to devise and implement a comprehensive strategy to manage and develop the relationship between America and China.

In theory, it should be possible to work out such a strategy. America is a rational and optimistic nation that has woven into its cultural and psychological fabric the highest traditions of Western humanist and rational thought. Open-mindedness is prized. But paradoxically, the deep American self-confidence in American openness presents an enormous obstacle to a viable long-term understanding with China. Hence, it is likely that America and China will at several points in the twenty-first century misunderstand each other.

The sources of misunderstanding could be many. Competition between nations has often been compared to chess games. Geopolitics is seen by analogy as just a complex chess game. For the past few hundred years, during the time that the leading powers have all been European, the only chess game they have played was Western chess. China, however, has its own chess game, called Chinese chess or Xiangqi. The end goal of the game is the same: to checkmate the king. But the players are different. So too is the format of the chess board and the nature of the moves across it. When America and China spend the next few decades adjusting to each other, it is quite conceivable that Americans will think that they are playing Western chess while the Chinese will think that they are playing Chinese chess.

The first source of misunderstanding between America and China will derive from their different national experiences. America, too, is culture-bound. It looks at the future through the prism of its own history. Since it emerged on the world stage, all the geopolitical rules of engagement and conflict between naval or friendly powers were set by European thinkers. World War I, World War II, and the Cold War were essentially Western geopolitical games, even though some of the players, like Japan, were non-Western.

Indeed, unwittingly, Japan may have contributed to some of the misunderstanding that surrounds the rise of China. From the very first days of the Meiji restoration in 1868, when Japan decided to modernize and develop itself, it had decided that the road to success was to emulate Western societies and be accepted by the Western club. Japan took on both the best and worst practices. It developed a first-rate economy, not once but twice in the twentieth century. But as it succeeded, it copied the European imperialist dynamic of expanding militarily and occupying weaker neighboring states. After having been defeated in World War II, it again obeyed faithfully the post-World War II rules of the game, developed a first-world economy and happily joined the powerful Western clubs, becoming the first Asian country to join groups like the Organisation for Economic Co-operation and Development (OECD) and G7. In doing so, Japan created a natural expectation in the West that any subsequent successful non-Western country would follow the path established and used not once but twice by Japan.

China will not. Superficially, China will behave like any other nation state, joining in and participating in various multilateral fora. But if China continues to succeed and develop in strength and emerges as a real great power, it will fall back on its own distinct history in determining the role it will carve out for itself in the world. For such a large country as China, it is surprising that China has a minimal imperial tradition outside its borders. Throughout the period of the European Dark Ages, China became powerful at several points. Indeed the peak of Chinese civilization was probably reached as early as the eighth century A.D. with the Tang Dynasty. In all these periods, China could have easily expanded its empire beyond its borders but it expressed no desire to do so. It was happy to receive tributes from its neighbors and be acknowledged as "The Middle Kingdom" or, implicitly, as the center of the universe.

Unlike Japan in the early twentieth century, China will feel a lesser compulsion to expand militarily to demonstrate its power. It will not compete with America in developing a huge navy with several aircraft carriers to project its military power in every corner of the world. After the military humiliations of the past two centuries, China will certainly develop and maintain a strong military capacity to defend itself. But when its power grows, it will be confident that other countries, beginning with Asian countries on its periphery, will begin to acknowledge China once more as "The Middle Kingdom." When that happens, China will feel that it has once again arrived. The envoys arriving in Beijing bearing political and psychological tributes will mark the restoration of China's place in the world.

Hard-headed American thinkers, especially those who belong to the culturally dominant "realist" school of strategic thinkers, will scoff at the suggestion that cultural recognition as number one can satisfactorily replace military dominance. These thinkers are culturally programmed to believe that China will behave like a normal European power and engage in a military, not a cultural or political, race with America. And since many of these thinkers have dominated American policymaking in recent decades, they have planted in many key American institutions an ingrained tendency to see China as the real big "threat": namely that when China succeeds, it will engage in a major military contest with America. Hence, in some of these circles there is an understandable desire to plot and plan ways and means of tripping China up before it becomes a rival military power to the United States (including plans to push for greater democracy in Hong Kong and Taiwan to embarrass or spread political ferment in the Chinese mainland).

It is conceivable that when (and not if) China emerges as a great power, it will behave like a normal European power and seek military domination. But a recent example illustrates how differently the Chinese typically respond.

After America had withdrawn from Vietnam, the victorious Vietnamese leaders in Hanoi succumbed to one of the oldest human failings: arrogance. Ignoring the long history of Sino-Vietnamese relations (which had lasted two thousand years), Vietnam in December 1978 invaded a neighboring state, Cambodia, against explicit Chinese warnings. China had no choice but to retaliate militarily against Vietnam, despite the risk of a military retaliation from Vietnam's ally, the Soviet Union. China did not occupy any Vietnamese territory. Instead it launched a punitive military incursion into Vietnam (albeit a massive one) and then withdrew. Military scholars are still debating who actually won the military battles on the ground, Vietnam or China. Probably the Vietnamese military performed better. But the military debate is irrelevant. China accomplished its goal of forcing Vietnam to tie down 600,000 troops to defend the Sino-Vietnamese border, which from 1979 to 1990 was probably among the most heavily mined and fortified borders in the world.

In 1985, in the middle of this period, I was invited to Columbia University to give a lecture on Vietnam and its neighbors. When I arrived at the lecture room, I discovered three Vietnamese diplomats sitting in the front row. This was somewhat disconcerting as I had planned to say things that they would not find pleasing. I thought that they might dispute my description of a recurrent aspect of Sino-Vietnamese military relations: namely, that while the Vietnamese had from time to time defeated invading Chinese armies, they had always, thereafter, sent emissaries to Beijing bearing tributes to "apologize" for having defeated the Chinese invaders. I then added that the real mistake made by the Vietnamese in 1979 was not necessarily to defeat the Chinese armies but their failure to send emissaries to Beijing to apologize for doing so. To my surprise, as I said this, the three Vietnamese diplomats began to nod their heads in agreement.

What followed subsequently in the Sino-Vietnamese relationship confirmed the assessment that the longer history of Sino-Vietnamese relations, not the contemporary European balance-of-power assumptions, would dictate the outcome. After the collapse of its ally, the Soviet Union, in 1991, Vietnam knew that it would have no choice but to make peace with China. It withdrew from Cambodia and began to send envoys to Beijing. The restoration of the traditional patterns of Sino-Vietnamese relations changed everything. The mines and fortifications were removed from the previously impenetrable hostile border. Almost overnight it went from zero trade to one of the busiest meeting places for cross-border exchange. All "sins" were quickly forgiven when the traditional relationship was restored between China and Vietnam.

Americans who want to understand the significance of this remarkable transformation of the Sino-Vietnamese relationship from total hostility to normal neighborliness in a short period of time should ask themselves a simple question: Why does it take America so long to reconcile itself with its erstwhile enemies or adversaries? As a people, Americans are among the most compassionate and forgiving. Individual Americans are big-hearted. Yet, as a polity, America is one of the most unforgiving countries of the world. It seems incapable of emulating what China accomplished with Vietnam.

Three examples illustrate this point. Vietnam is the first and most obvious. After the collapse of the Soviet Union in 1991, America quickly made peace with Russia and virtually all the pro-Soviet countries who signaled a willingness to reach a new accommodation with America. Vietnam sent similar overtures. It was rebuffed. The memory of having been defeated in 1975 was still vivid in American minds. No American politician dared to take the bold statesmanlike road of making peace with a former enemy that was no longer a threat. The normalization of relations with Vietnam had to wait several years and was finally carried out quietly on July 11, 1995, and a visit by President Clinton had to wait until November 16, 2000, when he no longer had to worry about re-election.

America's attitude to Cuba is just as rigid and unforgiving. Castro is by no means a threat to America. He is at best an irritation. Most observers believe normalization of relations with Cuba would only undermine Castro's government, because a free flow of American tourists, money, and information would create new opportunities for the population of Cuba. But here again few American politicians have been brave enough to take the statesman-like road of advocating normal relations with Cuba, in the way that China achieved with Vietnam. The domestic Cuban constituency in Florida is politically mighty. It dictates the terms of American engagement with Cuba. Hence the perception that any normalization between America and Cuba would be seen in America as a political victory for Castro even though one is an ant and the other is an elephant.

Iran is the third example of America's inability to forgive. One of the most humiliating moments of recent American history was the day that American diplomats were taken hostage by Khomeini's government in 1979. Iran was ostracized for a generation. But the Iranian government eventually began to transform itself. After democratic elections, several moderate leaders were elected to key posts, including President Khatami. Undoubtedly, much of the political power still rested with the religious conservatives. But there was a genuine longing among many Iranians to break free from the Khomeini era and join the modern world. Americans could have aided the process by "forgiving" Iran and establishing normal diplomatic relations. Normal diplomatic relations do not in any way imply approval of a government, just as American diplomatic relations with Brezhnev's Soviet Union or Ceausescu's Romania did not signify approval of those regimes. Yet till today the American polity is unable to forgive Iran for having had the audacity to hold American diplomats hostage.

These examples illustrate a key paradox that will bedevil the Sino-American relationship as both sides struggle to find a stable long-term modus vivendi. The paradox is this. Over the long term, there is no doubt that America will be the more stable political actor. American governance is both stable and adaptable to change. The rule of law is well-established. This is why billions of dollars are still invested in America. The American system can provide political and economic stability across generations. The imperial rulers of China devised a political system that served China more or less well for over two thousand years, but this system of imperial rule, based on a "mandate of heaven," crashed at the beginning of the twentieth century. A hundred years later China is struggling to find an equally viable long-term alternative. This is not surprising: Two-thousand-year-old political systems cannot be transformed overnight. China may well take another hundred years to find a viable long-term solution. We can reasonably predict the state of the American political system a hundred years from now but we cannot do the same for China.

Despite this reality, it is paradoxically easier to predict Chinese political behavior over the short-term than American political behavior. Although it is frequently said that dictatorships are more predictable than democracies, Chinese dependability is based on well-rehearsed statecraft for over two thousand years. There is a great deal of accumulated wisdom within the inner sanctums of Beijing, similar to the political wisdom accumulated for over a thousand years within the walls of the Vatican. This political wisdom explains how China managed to remain a fairly stable and predictable external actor through some of its most disastrous domestic eras in recent times, including the Great Leap Forward, the Cultural Revolution, and the rise of the Gang of Four. Secretary of State Henry Kissinger arrived in Beijing in 1971, not long after China had emerged from the throes of the Cultural Revolution. Yet the two individuals he met were probably the most sophisticated interlocutors whom he would have to deal with in his life: Zhou En-Lai and Mao Zedong. In China, leaders may come and go. But the political instincts developed to handle the outside world have been honed over centuries. No Chinese leaders would ever express it publicly but secretly many believe that the arrival of American power at their doorstep is no different from the arrival of the many other barbarians who had come to China only to be eventually absorbed within the cosmos of Chinese civilization.

American political behavior, by contrast, is almost akin to that of a nouveau riche person who has just been admitted to a long-established country club. He flashes his wealth and power but has not troubled to learn the customs and values of the club that he has gained admission to.

American foreign policies are unpredictable because they are the result of a complex set of factors and actors: special interest groups, popular (often populist) opinions, media biases, and the changing electoral dynamics. When a new American president is elected, even with a strong mandate, his capacity to change the fundamental directions of American domestic policies is limited. There are several checks and balances within the American political system and divisions of power even within the executive. By contrast there are fewer restraints placed on the power of the American president in global society: his capacity to change the course of international relations is much greater than his capacity to change domestic policy, which must be approved by the Senate and House.

Even a country as big and as ancient as China has to bob and weave whenever a new American president is elected. The paradox here is that the American system of electing its president every four years is designed to produce domestic stability over the long term. But, despite the benign intentions of America's founding fathers, it is a system that has come to generate instability on the international scene. An interesting statistic is that almost every new U.S. president goes to war somewhere—often in his first year in office. Over the course of the past few decades, Chinese officials have resigned themselves to the fact that they have to spend some time "educating" a new administration when it comes to office. Over time, China will hone its skills, just as Tony Blair was able to move effortlessly from being the closest friend of Bill Clinton to becoming the closest friend of George W. Bush. But until that happens, we can anticipate unpredictable U.S.-China relations.

There are no shortages of specific political issues that could either bedevil or be used to bedevil the Sino-American relationship: from Tibet to Taiwan, from North Korea to the South China Sea. Each has a specific history and structure and is also a piece on the complex Sino-American chessboard. Until the larger context is understood, none of these specific issues can be properly understood.

Tibet, fortunately, now appears to be the least combustible. Despite the immense personal popularity of the Dalai Lama in the Western world, where he has achieved almost cult-like status, most political analysts recognize that independence for Tibet is a non-starter. The possibility of China ceding control over Tibet is as likely as the U.S. ceding control of New Mexico to Mexico. Hence, the political temperature of the Tibet issue has subsided significantly in recent years.

Those who try to argue for the preservation and continued development of Tibetan culture, which is both unique and impressive, have a case. If China could develop greater confidence in the benign intentions of those who act as spokespersons for Tibetan culture, there could be greater scope for cooperation with China in this area. But China now views warily any such defenders of Tibetan culture as covert advocates of independence for Tibet.

Bill Clinton once remarked that one of his biggest regrets was his failure to secure a face-to-face meeting between Jiang Zemin, then President of China, and the Dalai Lama. Clinton said he tried hard and he felt that he almost succeeded. But in the final analysis, Jiang Zemin had felt that he could not take the political risk. Many Americans will be puzzled by Jiang's unwillingness to meet a major religious and cultural figure like the Dalai Lama, especially since the Dalai Lama is known to be a strong advocate of nonviolence. But the political risk to Jiang Zemin was akin to the risk Bill Clinton took in meeting Fidel Castro. Clinton did shake hands with Castro, quickly and briefly during an U.N. lunch hosted by Kofi Annan, but only when no American journalists or cameramen were present. American political leaders face serious constraints in taking bold political initiatives. So do Chinese leaders, who in some ways have to work harder because they must preserve not only their popularity but also the very legitimacy of their leadership.

China today is like a dragon waking up after centuries of slumber, waking up to realize that many others have been trampling on its territory while it has been asleep. Given all that has happened to China over the past two centuries, it would not have been surprising if indeed China had awoken as an angry dragon. Instead, what we see emerging in China is a nation that has no desire to play a disruptive role on the world stage. In part this is a result of China's awareness of its current relative weakness and in part a result of China's relatively peaceful history with its neighbors. But it is also because China has believed the vision presented by America after World War II: that nations need no longer pursue paths of military conquest to grow and prosper. Instead, trade and economic integration provide a surer path to economic prosperity and peace. China has observed how well both Japan and Germany emerged from the ruins of World War II.

Taiwan is today politically a more difficult issue than Tibet. It still sits on the front burner and continues to face the risk of boiling over from time to time. The core American position on Taiwan recognizes that since the people of Taiwan have lived separately from the Chinese mainland since 1949, any effort to integrate them with the mainland should be done peacefully. At the same time, America opposes Taiwanese independence and recognizes the Chinese claim to sovereignty over Taiwan. This American position is reasonable.

Delicate American handling of the Taiwan issue has so far prevented it from becoming a major threat, though it has remained an irritant, in the Sino-American relationship. The Chinese government in the past never had any serious plans to take over Taiwan by military force and even today would be reluctant to do so. The wiser Chinese leaders realize that the continuing economic success of Taiwan can serve as a beacon of hope for the Chinese people, who naturally admire the success of overseas Chinese anywhere in the world. Also, with growing trade and economic links leading to closer economic integration, it will only be a matter of time before both sides reach a comfortable modus vivendi, just as the Republic of Ireland and the United Kingdom overcame the burden of their fractious history through closer integration within the European Union, which will in turn lay the political foundations of trust to resolve the Northern Ireland problem.

The Chinese leaders however believe, with some justification, that the Taiwan issue has been used from time to time as a means of pressuring the Chinese government. Americans can justifiably argue that they were not responsible for the rise of political parties in Taiwan that advocated independence. This was a natural and inevitable result of democratization and America, of all countries, could not block the emergence of such open democratic forces. It would place the United States in an ideologically awkward position. American policymakers do argue that they did not encourage pro-independence forces in Taiwan but the only reason why these pro-independence forces do not fear retaliation from China is because of solid American military protection. When China fired a few missiles to land off the shores of Taiwan in late 1995 as a carefully calibrated warning shot across the bow, and continued with another round of similar missile tests in early 1996, America responded by sending two aircraft carrier battle groups to the region in March 1996 (although many press reports misleadingly said that the aircraft carriers entered the Taiwan Straits; in actual fact they did not do so). The message was clear. America would not allow Taiwan to be bullied militarily. In short, while America may not have consciously encouraged the forces of Taiwanese independence, it had created the conditions for these forces to grow and flourish. It has also constrained China's capacity to react.

The twists and turns of the Taiwan issue are complex and deserve an entire book of their own. Each side can justify the positions that it takes. But as American officials immerse themselves in the daily details of the Taiwan issue, they often seem to ignore one huge reality: In the eyes of the Chinese leaders and the Chinese people, the continued separation of Taiwan from the mainland is the last relic of the humiliating era when China was trampled upon by invading powers. If America had not positioned itself as an absolute protector of Taiwan, both sides across the Taiwan Straits would have eventually reached a pragmatic compromise and learned to live with each other. Just as China quickly forgave Vietnam after the massive military conflict in 1979, China would have readily accepted a completely autonomous Taiwan that nominally accepted Chinese sovereignty. Such an offer still remains on the table.

The tragedy here is that the one Western country, America, that played virtually no role in humiliating China in the nineteenth and early twentieth centuries when other powers were trampling on it has emerged as the one power preserving the last relic of China's humiliation. Most sophisticated Chinese understand there is no conscious American desire to humiliate China or remind it of its past degradations. But each time America allows the forces of independence to grow or flourish in Taiwan, it pushes the Chinese leaders into a corner in which their political options become very limited. Several Chinese political leaders have made it clear that they would be lynched by their own populations and never forgiven by history if they allowed Taiwan to become independent. Even though it would be disastrous for China to launch a war with Taiwan (especially a war that would also lead to a military confrontation with America), the Chinese leaders have made it abundantly clear that they would have no choice but to do so if Taiwan were to declare its political independence from China.

Some American leaders have from time to time shown greater delicacy and sensitivity in handling the Taiwan issue. In early 2004, when President Chen Shui-bian of Taiwan unwisely decided to suggest that a referendum be held to assess the views of the Taiwanese people on independence, President George W. Bush sent a firm message to the Taiwanese leader that America did not approve of his actions. President Bush also reassured the Chinese leadership that America was *not* behind Chen Shui-bian's moves. This was wise statesmanship. But this wise statesmanship was also a result of America's geopolitical need for China's support on other more pressing issues, like Iraq and North Korea. Had 9/11 not happened, Sino-American relations might well have gone down a different road with the Taiwan issue occupying the center stage. So far the vicissitudes of recent history have prevented this, but the issue remains nevertheless a potentially volatile element in the Sino-American relationship. And the extent of the volatility is probably far greater than most American policymakers have ever imagined.

The danger of allowing the Taiwan issue to float is that America may be unintentionally unleashing forces of Chinese nationalism that may in turn force the Chinese government to take more belligerent postures. China is fortunate to have significant resources of political wisdom. But when nationalism is unleashed, conciliatory leaders can easily be swept away by uncontrollable domestic political forces.

It is an irony that since World War II America has provided the stable political and security framework that has allowed the East

Asian regions, including China, to grow and flourish. It would have been disastrous for the region if America had decided to pack up and go home immediately after World War II, a move that could well have happened given the traditional reluctance of the American body politic to get deeply immersed in foreign entanglements. Instead America stayed in the region and stayed on despite two wars. America lost over 35,000 lives in the Korean War and more than 50,000 lives in the Vietnam War. When fair and objective evaluations of the Pacific region in the second half of the twentieth century emerge, the record will show that the strong American military presence and the firm support it showed to its allies and friends was a crucial reason for the growth and success of the region. Without the open American market, neither Japan nor the four East Asian Tigers (Hong Kong, South Korea, Singapore, and Taiwan) would have grown so rapidly. Even China's economic success in the 1980s and 1990s was significantly assisted by open access to American markets.

Given the enormous beneficial effect that America has had upon the region since 1945, it would be tragic if America were to be ultimately remembered as the country that destabilized the region by mismanaging the rise and emergence of China. The recent emergence of anti-Americanism in many regions across the globe was much less marked, relatively speaking, in East Asia. Much goodwill remains. But unwise American policies could reverse that.

One of the most dangerous dimensions of American policy towards China is the strongly held belief among key American strategic thinkers that China would benefit enormously if it could be transformed into a democracy, the sooner, the better. A natural corollary of this belief is that anything that the United States can do either to plant the seeds of democracy or to allow the emergence of pro-democratic forces would therefore only benefit China. It is almost impossible to shake this conviction from American minds because it plays to the belief that America has become the most successful society in the history of man because it has the most democratic society in the world. This may be true for America. Even though America is probably the youngest nation among all the great powers, American thinkers believe that their openness is a universal panacea. If they could rid China of its "oppressive" Communist Party rule, China would grow and flourish after the forces of freedom had taken over.

It is not surprising then that the United States and China reached almost exactly opposite conclusions on the real effect of the collapse of the Communist Party rule in Soviet Union. Americans cheered the disappearance of the Communist Party. They cheered the arrival of democratic elections. Part of this was because the Soviet nuclear threat had terrorized American minds subconsciously for decades. Several American friends of mine told me that they slept much better when the Soviet nuclear missiles were no longer controlled by the Communist Party (even though ironically the Soviet Communist Party had been rational and predictable in its behavior for decades). It was also assumed that freedom would inevitably improve the living conditions of the Russians. Few Americans noticed the implosion of the Russian economy, the rapid impoverishment of millions, and the remarkable deterioration in key indicators of social and economic well-being, including life expectancy and infant mortality. The Russian people did.

While Americans observed the explosion of freedom in Russia after Communist Party rule ended, the Chinese leaders and people witnessed both the destruction of Soviet power, the quick collapse of the Soviet state, and the anarchy that was experienced by the poorer classes. The wealth of the Russian state was transferred not to the people but to a few oligarchs. Corruption rose. Hence, when the Chinese looked at Russia in the 1990s, it reminded them of some of the painful decades they experienced in the early twentieth century, when both corruption and anarchy were endemic. The Chinese leaders shuddered at the prospect of this happening in China. Indeed the greatest danger that Chinese political thinkers have warned against has always been *Luan* (chaos). After watching what happened in Russia, the Chinese leadership (and probably a wide range of elites) reached the conclusion that Chinese Communist Party rule would be needed for a decade or more.

It is virtually impossible to convince any American that the continuation of Chinese Communist Party rule—of the kind seen since Deng Xiaoping launched the modernization of China—would be good for China, good for America, and good for the world. Good Communist Party rule is dismissed by Americans as an oxymoron. After witnessing the painful experience of the Balkans following the export of democracy and the removal of the Communist Party in Yugoslavia, some Americans might reluctantly concede that in some circumstances Communist Party rule may indeed be a lesser evil. But good it could never be.

A rigid adherence to ideology can create its own blindness. In the last decade or more, while Americans have preserved in their minds an unchanging vision of the Chinese Communist Party, they have failed to take note of its remarkable transformation. On paper it looks like the same political animal. In reality, the party is now completely different. Never before has China assembled such a broad sophisticated elite to manage the affairs of its state. Many have been trained overseas. When Americans try to envision Communist Party officials, they visualize old party hacks like Brezhnev and Gromyko. But if they were to travel to China and meet the Communist Party leaders running key cities, for example, they will meet young Chinese mayors, many of whom have Harvard or Stanford MBAs: Mayor Han Zheng of Shanghai (49 years old); Mayor Li Hongzhong of Shenzhen (46 years old), and Vice-Mayor Lu Hao of Beijing (35 years old).

After more than a hundred years of anarchy and misrule, China has finally amassed the best governing class it has seen in generations. There are no aging commissars clinging on to party rule. Instead, there is a set of leaders committed to moving China forward. The success of their policies is evident. It is hard enough to deliver rapid economic growth in small- or medium-sized societies. To watch the most populous society in the world experiencing the most rapid economic growth is like seeing the fattest boy in class winning the 100-meter hurdle race. Despite all the enormous baggage it carries socially, culturally, politically, the Chinese economy has outpaced almost every other economy in the past two decades. This does not happen naturally. It requires incredibly deft economic management, of a kind delivered by China's new sophisticated elite.

China is no paradise. It has enormous flaws. Large pools of poverty remain. Corruption is widespread, especially at local levels. There is often brutal and arbitrary rule in provinces where the checks from the center are less frequent. Any American reporter looking for flaws in the Chinese social and political fabric will find many, and that is why there is no shortage of negative stories on China in the American media. In the world's largest society, it may even be natural to find the largest number of flaws. But if instead of taking a static view of China, we compare China's overall position today to where it has been in the past two centuries, there can be no doubt that the Chinese people are far better off today.

In its dealings with foreign nations, especially the Western world, it may seem wiser for China to abandon all pretense that it is run by a Communist Party. China today is far more capitalist than communist. In the early 1980s, when I first visited China, I would walk into a hotel room, open a drawer, and find a little red book of Mao's sayings, a gesture similar to the Western hotel practice of leaving a Bible for use by guests. A decade later, in the early 1990s, the little red book of Mao had been replaced by glossy economic brochures that explained to the visitor why he or she should invest in that particular province or city. A fierce competition for private investment had broken out among Chinese cities and provinces: China had become a paradise for visiting capitalists, who could enjoy enormous competition for their investment dollars. Indeed if the initials CPC were retained and stood for "Capitalist Party of China" rather than "Communist Party of China," it might be a fairer description of the ruling party's economic policies.

Those visiting capitalists who delighted in the glossy economic brochures have irreversibly linked China's economy with businesses all over the world. Thomas Friedman summarized the new interdependence: "The relationship of the world to China right now reminds me of that old banker's rule: If a client owes you $1,000, that's his problem. If a client owes you $1 million, that's your problem. China's stability is our problem."[1]

It would be disastrous for China to suddenly disband the Communist Party. Political legitimacy is a very valuable but also a very fragile commodity. The Communist Party does enjoy legitimacy in China. Most Western scholars, when they remember Mao Zedong, think of the excesses and disasters of Mao's rule. The Chinese recognize the deep flaws of his era but they also know that it took a man of steel like Mao to reunify China and put it back on the track of national unity and growth. If Mao had not come along, China could well have taken a century or more to regain national unity and a sense of purpose. The current verdict of Western scholarship on Mao's rule is unlikely to be the ultimate verdict of Chinese scholars. The Chinese perception of a historical cycle is longer than in the Western view. It is said that when the writer André Malraux visited China in the 1960s in his capacity as the French minister of culture, he asked Zhou En-Lai what he thought of the French Revolution of 1789. Zhou replied that it was too early to tell.

There is no more contentious issue than the Cultural Revolution of the 1960s, an immensely painful period of China in which many innocent people suffered. Both educated people and party cadres were sent to toil in the countryside. Millions died. Families were split asunder. Many Chinese who have emigrated to the United States have described in vivid detail the sufferings they went through. Take for example Nien Cheng, author of *Life and Death in Shanghai*, and Ji-Li Jiang, author of *Red Scarf Girl*. There is a vast, and for Western readers, self-justifying literature of Chinese families who have suffered and escaped the Cultural Revolution. Unsurprisingly, books celebrating the Cultural Revolution have proved less popular. Instead, the popularity of dissident accounts has influenced the perceptions of American intellectuals towards China. They see the Cultural Revolution as an unmitigated disaster.

But was it? It is a great struggle for any society to free itself from feudalism. China had experienced four thousand years of feudalism. In the course of these four thousand years, the peasants assumed that their lot in life was to remain at the bottom of the social ladder. By the time Mao's rule ended, the pride and self-confidence of the peasant class had been uplifted. Singapore experienced this at first hand. Singapore allows women from neighboring countries to work as housekeepers for Singapore families. Traditionally, Singaporeans recruited housekeepers from the Philippines, Indonesia, and Sri Lanka. When our Filipino housekeeper went to the crowded markets with my American-born wife, Anne, she would drive Anne crazy because she would insist on walking a few steps behind the lady of the house, never side by side. Feudalism is still deeply entrenched in the Philippines. This may also help to explain why it is struggling to develop even though it is the only country to have been colonized by America for fifty years. One year, we decided, as an experiment, to employ a housekeeper from one of the poorest provinces of China, Anhui. Her name was Zi Yun. Anne was delighted to discover that Zi Yun immediately walked side by side with her in the markets. She came from a poor province in China but had great cultural self-confidence and pride. One reasonable question that can be asked is whether the economic explosion we have seen in China could have taken place if the vast majority of the peasant classes had not had their pride, dignity, and sense of self worth uplifted by the Communist revolution? To have given the poor of China a significant boost in their sense of self-esteem and psychological confidence is no small achievement on the part of the Communist Party.

The Communist Party has also retained its legitimacy in recent decades by constantly reinventing itself. Heraclitus once said we can never step into the same river twice. Similarly we can never step twice into the same Communist Party of China. It is constantly changing. China is lucky that the CPC produced not one but two towering giants in the twentieth century. One was Mao. The other was Deng Xiaoping. I have no doubt that Deng Xiaoping will eventually be recognized as the greatest leader of China, perhaps the greatest leader of the twentieth century. He inherited the Communist Party from Mao, who had tried to launch the most thoroughgoing of all Communist Party revolutions by eliminating the feudal landlords and capitalist classes. Deng used the same Communist Party to turn the huge country of China on a dime. He turned it sharply away from Communist Party economic controls and took massive steps towards the free market system. Through all this he preserved political stability in China. Deng's legacy will always be dogged by the Tiananmen tragedy. However, Chinese scholars will view this tragedy against the larger backdrop of Chinese history and understand why Deng had to retain firm political control. If Deng had lost his nerve in Tiananmen, China could have wasted decades trying to regain its sense of drive and purpose.

Deng also laid down the guidelines for Communist Party leadership: Select only the best. Have a program of constant self-renewal. Indeed, Deng could just as well have said: Learn from Harvard. Harvard is ruthlessly meritocratic. It takes a top-down, not bottom-up, approach to appointing professors. It will not appoint any professor until it is convinced that it has found the best possible person for the job. The CPC does the same. It has developed equally rigorous ways and means of assessing and deploying talent. Indeed, several of China's newest leaders are Harvard-educated, including Li Hongzhong, mayor of rapidly growing Shenzhen.

It is inherently difficult for the American mind to conceive that non-democratic rule of China has worked—perhaps better than a premature democracy ever could have. Americans fervently believe that democracy is the best possible form of government, both for ideological and for pragmatic reasons. Apart from the strong sense of ownership of the society that is generated in any citizenry that is allowed to both select and remove its rulers, democracy is also extremely functional because it provides a ready "flushing" mechanism to remove incompetent, corrupt, or unpopular leaders. This explains the energy and vitality of the American ruling elite. Every four or eight years, a new team arrives in the capital to provide fresh leadership, ideas, and direction. No other capital in the world, not even those of other developed Western countries, enjoys the same degree of renewal and revitalization of its ruling elite.

China has no such blessing. It will take a long time before China enjoys the kind of democratic rule that America enjoys, perhaps a century or more. But this does not mean that China cannot replicate the *results* of the American political system within the Chinese political system. The means may be different. The CPC will follow the Harvard system rather than the Iowa caucus system. But if the CPC develops a disciplined set of rules and a healthy corporate culture and installs the right people to carry out the selection processes, it may well be able to match America in producing a vibrant and dynamic elite. Indeed, given the demoralization that occasionally affects government bureaucracies in America because of their inability to pay salaries competitive with the private sector, it is conceivable that many Chinese officials doing the same job as their American counterparts may be more gifted and talented (although China still has a long way to go to match the wealth of talent in the larger American establishment).

Americans understand meritocracy well. There is fierce competition in the sports arena, whether it be in football or baseball, basketball or ice hockey. No institution will select its second or third team to represent it in any sports competition. But this is what America occasionally does with its civil service. It does not select the brightest American minds, most of whom choose to go into the more lucrative private or professional sectors. Fortunately some of them go on to serve in political positions and provide leadership and drive. China, by contrast, is learning to field its first team in most of its government agencies. New York City is still the world's capital. It attracts the best talent from all over the world. The talent pool in New York City is unrivaled. Shanghai cannot match it, yet. But the bureaucratic agencies that run Shanghai are often staffed by more able officials than their New York counterparts. The physical infrastructure of New York is decaying; that of Shanghai is sparkling. Soon, the cultural and intellectual infrastructure of Shanghai could be equally sparkling, if China gradually allows an increasing degree of political openness.

The Chinese system of non-democratic rule cannot work over the long run. Without the means to prevent the emergence of corrupt and static elites, there is always a great danger that China could again lapse into the sort of corrupt rule that China has seen before. China will have to adapt and move towards democracy. Indeed this will be one of the biggest challenges for China in this and the next century. But although China will have to change over the long term, this does not mean that the current Chinese system is not viable and effective for the short term. The sense of time varies from society to society. For Americans, two centuries is a long time. It represents almost the entire duration of the republic. For the Chinese two centuries is a short time. Hence, the current Chinese system may well be viable for a century or more.

Given the current strength and legitimacy of the CPC, it is fortunate that there is no conscious American policy to overturn or remove it. But America happily supports Chinese dissidents or religious movements like the Falun Gong on the assumption that any expansion of "freedom" in the Chinese political space can only be good for China. If such activities destabilize the Chinese political system, it surely proves that the political system is wrong. If the political system collapses as a result of the flourishing of these dissident activities, it could only be a positive outcome. None of this is articulated explicitly because the ideological assumptions are so deeply embedded. One of the goals of this book is to encourage Americans to revisit the ideological assumptions they use to understand the rest of the world. The twenty-first century will be immensely different from the nineteenth and twentieth centuries. Americans are only disadvantaging themselves if they believe that the ideological perspectives of the past two centuries, even those that have served them well over these past two centuries, are sufficient to help them understand the different world of the twenty-first century.

One ideological premise that should be discarded is the belief that the removal of any undemocratic regime can only lead to good, not harm. In the real world, many countries are held together by politically weak regimes, which have to forge untidy and difficult compromises to sustain the unity of the country. Their removal need not lead to the people being better off. In this regard, the decapitation of the Saddam Hussein regime may provide the world with a live laboratory experiment on the management of regime change. Saddam Hussein was a vile and corrupt ruler. His removal was a blessing for the Iraqi people. No tears need to be shed for him. But the subsequent steps of totally eliminating the Iraqi army and expelling all Baath Party members effectively tore down some key pillars that were holding Iraqi society together. Restoring some degree of political stability and unity to Iraq will be an enormous challenge. The Iraqi political experiment may or may not succeed but the period of political transition will be painful for the Iraqi people and perhaps unleash new forces that were quiescent (and perhaps best left quiescent).

A sudden end to Communist Party rule in China at this point would prove even more disastrous and painful, for the people of China, the people of the region, and indeed the world as a whole. There are strong populist and nationalist forces within the Chinese political fabric. They are carefully controlled and managed by the skilled political leadership of the CPC. If these populist forces were ever unleashed, the nationalism that might emerge and confront the world in the twenty-first century may well be angrier and more difficult to manage. Hence, the CPC may well be doing the world an enormous favor by managing the gradual but positive transformation of Chinese society and steering it in the direction of integrating with the new globalized society as a responsible citizen. The whole world has a vested interest in the success of this great Chinese experiment. America must become a constructive, not an antagonistic, stakeholder in it.

America also needs to understand the enormous impact of its actions on other countries. Even societies as large as China's can be affected by American moves. Americans believe that no harm can be done if they support political dissidents. They believe that they are only helping individuals in distress, not trying to damage or shake a political system. By contrast the Chinese leadership is acutely aware that in this period of political transition as they try to move from Communist Party rule to a more open and representative political system, they will be moving through treacherous political territory. The political ground they are walking on is very unsteady. Indeed it is almost like climbing up a mountain slope filled with loose rocks which, if they are loosened suddenly, could trigger an avalanche that could sweep them away. As they try clambering up this treacherous slope, they find Americans throwing little rocks at their feet. They hear the verbal assurances by American leaders that America is not trying to politically destabilize China. Yet they can also see the deeds: support of dissidents, encouragement of nationalist forces in Taiwan, the lionization of the Dalai Lama. All these actions can impact China's political stability.

After several decades of close encounters with Americans, the Chinese leaders have developed a reasonably sophisticated feel of how to work with America. They now know that argument alone will not be enough to persuade America to be more careful and restrained in carrying out actions that impact on China. China has learned that America, like any other country, responds when its own national interests are directly affected. It serves Chinese interests to see the emergence of situations when America needs Chinese assistance. This happens whenever America gets into political trouble. Each time America does so, it develops an interest in seeking China's cooperation. It then serves China's interests to calibrate its cooperation to reflect America's behavior towards China at that moment. It would be foolish to underestimate China's ability to play delicate geopolitical games, requiring deft political footwork.

Two recent issues that have preoccupied American leaders, Iraq and North Korea, have demonstrated Chinese diplomatic dexterity. When America announced its decision to launch a military invasion of Iraq, China, as a matter of principle, had to oppose it. Unlike France, which tried hard to prevent America's invasion of Iraq,

China did so quietly. Perhaps China did not want to aggravate the American leadership. But could it also have been because of a sophisticated Chinese calculation that an American invasion of Iraq would lead to America being stuck in a protracted and difficult overseas commitment? An America caught in an Iraqi quagmire would have less energy and ability to add to China's challenges.

Such an America would also need China's assistance in gatherings such as the U.N. Security Council. When America came back to the Security Council several months after the war began in an effort to secure legitimacy for its occupation and rule of Iraq, the Security Council agreed unanimously in Resolution No. 1511. A remarkable number of diplomatic twists and turns preceded the passage of this resolution; through these twists and turns China played a quietly helpful role which was much appreciated in Washington.

Similarly, when America decided to ratchet up the pressure on North Korea by declaring that North Korea was part of "the axis of evil," the Chinese probably anticipated that given the difficult and unpredictable nature of the North Korean regime, America would eventually seek China's assistance to persuade the North Korean leader to be more cooperative. That is exactly what happened. After releasing a lot of verbal bluster on North Korea, America discovered that it had few real levers to exert pressure. Bilateral economic sanctions would not work: North Korea had already isolated itself. Nor was military invasion feasible. The price that South Korea, and possibly Japan, would have paid from a military conflict would have been too high. The North Korean economy has been badly crippled but despite this, the North Korean military machine remains formidable. Hence when America needed to assert influence over North Korea, only one country had "persuasive" powers: China. America asked for help and China responded positively. Indeed, at one stage, in a powerful message of its serious intentions, China, virtually the sole supplier of oil to North Korea, cut off its oil supplies to North Korea for a few days.

The North Korean issue is politically complex. It has many dimensions. But when America decided that the denuclearization of the Korean peninsula was a national priority, it also created a certain degree of dependence on China. And it serves Chinese interests to increase, not reduce, such American dependence on China. By assisting America, China can restrain America from exerting pressure on China in the areas of China's own political vulnerabilities.

Iraq and North Korea are important. But they are dwarfed by another issue where eventually China can be very helpful to America's interests. In this one area, China's help can reach metaphysical proportions: its relations with the Islamic World. Given the deep and growing divide between Americans and Islam (despite the appearance of good ties between America and some Islamic governments), America cannot walk into the Islamic world now and be perceived as a positive agent for change. The Islamic world has become very suspicious of America.

By contrast, the Islamic world has no deep historical suspicion of China. There has never been a deep divide between China and Islam, despite the enormous differences in culture. There have been many encounters between China and Islam but the contacts have not been deep. Even though China has a sizeable Muslim population of its own (which has been restive from time to time), this Muslim minority has not dictated the terms of China's engagement with the Islamic world. As a consequence, without any historical baggage in their relationship (unlike, say, Islam with Christianity and the Crusades), there is no natural antipathy between Islam and China. Instead, there has long been admiration of the great Chinese civilization within the Islamic world.

If China successfully modernizes, its success may have a powerful ripple effect throughout the Islamic world. Many Islamic thinkers are reluctant to use the West as a model for Islam to emulate (even though in private many admit that they must match the West in education and science and technology). But these same thinkers would have no hesitation to use China as a positive example. China's success could lead to its becoming a beacon of hope, with Islamic scholars visiting Beijing to learn from Chinese civilization, as indeed they have done in centuries past. The Prophet Mohamed once said: "Seek knowledge, even into China. That is the duty for every Muslim."[2]

One of America's greatest strengths is its spirit of pragmatism. But this pragmatism is evident mostly in its day-to-day work, at the micro level. Americans should consider being a little less ideological and a little more pragmatic at a much higher level. Instead of viewing China's rise as a threat to America and its long-term interests, Americans should consider the possibility that it may have a major and positive catalytic effect on the rest of the world's population, especially the Islamic world. America's short-term geopolitical interest may not be served by a resurgent China. But America's stake in a more peaceful global community may be well served by a successful China providing a beacon of hope for the Islamic world, especially since the United States has ruled itself out as a possible beacon-bearer. Is there sufficient wisdom within the American body politic to both see and realize this? And is the American political system sophisticated enough to balance short-term against long-term interests? These are the sorts of questions that the rest of the world is now asking about America.

~ 5 ~

The Nature of American Power

THERE IS A WONDERFULLY VIVID American expression: "in your face." It describes vividly how a person feels when his personal space and often sense of personal dignity has been violated. It also describes how the 6 billion citizens outside America feel about American power. I once had the unfortunate experience of having the tire of a friend's car roll over my toes. I screamed. My friend, the driver, looked puzzled and immediately stopped the car, with the tire parked on my toes. It took me a while to explain the problem to him, and he of course rolled back the car with profound apologies. This is how many people feel about American power. It is parked on their toes. When they scream about it, they see only bewildered looks on the faces of their American friends, who are genuinely puzzled by the rising levels of anti-Americanism around the globe. Many Americans want to believe that all this is due to what they perceive as the insensitive and hard-headed policies of the Bush administration, but in fact the real

leave these global tentacles intact after the demise of the Soviet Union was a major decision. But there was no debate or discussion of this enormous decision. Instead, all Americans, both policymakers and the informed public, felt reflexively that American power, which they believed to be inherently benign, should maintain its global presence and not return to American shores.

It is also generally believed that American power can never be abused because of the extensive system of checks and balances that are placed on the American government by the American constitution. No one can wield absolute power within America. Hence, no American could wield American power absolutely outside America. The reality is that many of the checks and balances designed by the American constitution stop at the water's edge. If there was any doubt about this, Guantanamo confirmed it. It showed that American law did not even cover an American military base a few miles off shore.

Guantanamo had a profound effect on America's best friends overseas, the liberal elites. Many of these liberal elites may have had their own criticisms of America but they did believe that America was still the best society in the world in one critical respect: America believed that every human being, no matter what his status, had certain inalienable rights. Criminals in America, including those who had committed heinous crimes, enjoyed more rights than ordinary citizens in many parts of the globe. The rule of law was supreme in America. No one stood above the law in America, not even the American president. In this area, America was truly well ahead of the rest of the world. Before 9/11, even illegal migrants enjoyed some degree of rights in America. If any criminal anywhere in the world had been asked the question which legal authority he would like to be caught by, he would have probably said "America" because he would have had great legal protection. Indeed, as a young man, I often heard my friends say, "These Americans are nuts. They even give their criminals so many rights." But, at the same time, they would also show a grudging respect for a society that treated every human being with equal respect.

This is why Guantanamo was so shocking to so many. For the first time (in the eyes of many), American soldiers arrested some human beings and declared that they had no legal rights. A very special legal vacuum was created for them. American criminals had access to American courts; the Guantanamo detainees had none. Given the enormous checks and balances developed within America, many intellectuals in the rest of the world expected a large hue and cry over the creation of this legal vacuum under American authority. Instead, they noticed, in particular, the silence of the most hallowed American institutions, including the Supreme Court, and even the most liberal newspapers like the *New York Times*. On October 16, 2003, more than two years after 9/11, the *New York Times* finally criticized America's policy at Guantanamo: "The men held at Guantanamo are prisoners of the United States. While they may not have the same rights as American citizens, they should be treated in the highest tradition of American justice. That means they must be given some forum in which to contest their imprisonment, and there must be reasonable rules and some individualized proof for the detentions to be upheld."[2] 9/11 was such a shock to the American psyche that after two years Americans were just waking up from it. Instinctively, America had suspended the rule of law that had been its hallmark.

In human terms, the reaction of American society to 9/11 was perfectly understandable. America had been attacked by a vast and shadowy terrorist network, Al-Qaeda, which had developed cells around the world. America was not fighting a regular army. The regular rules of battle did not apply. Nor did the laws of war associated with the various Geneva conventions. The feeling in the American government therefore was that America had to create new rules and norms to deal with the new category of "non-military combatants." America did develop new practices. The mistake America made was not to develop new rules to both explain and justify these new practices. In so doing, American authorities were for the first time allowing the arbitrary use of power.

In some ways, Guantanamo may have had a more profound effect on the perceptions of intellectuals overseas of American power than Abu Ghraib did. Horrible things happened in Abu Ghraib, perhaps even more horrible than what Americans saw in the pictures. As a Jordanian diplomat explained to me, in both American and Western eyes, the worst "torture" that could be inflicted upon an individual was physical pain. But in the non-Western world, the worst "torture" was psychological. Disrobing an Arab completely and then forcing him into a sexual position on top of his nude son was far worse than any physical pain. This spiritual violation was more damaging than physical pain. Still, when evidence of atrocities in Abu Ghraib leaked out, American society reacted with enormous outrage. The checks and balances designed to prevent such atrocities came into play. President Bush spoke for the American people when he said, "I shared a deep disgust that these prisoners were treated the way they were treated. Their treatment does not reflect the nature of the American people."[3] Indeed, Abu Ghraib, paradoxically, may have re-established some of the respect for America as it showed how open and transparent the American system was. In many countries, atrocities committed by their troops are covered up. America showed that it believed in disclosure and accountability.

However, the outrage over Abu Ghraib only made the silence over Guantanamo even more noticeable. This silence in turn has affected perceptions of America. The Tiananmen incident of 1989, when many Chinese students were killed or imprisoned with brutal force, has been almost universally condemned in America. Most Americans felt that they had earned the moral right to make such criticisms because Americans would never treat human life as callously as the Chinese did. For most of the 1990s, the Chinese intellectuals, even if they did not agree fully with the substance of the American criticisms of Tiananmen, did not challenge the American moral authority in making such criticisms. Americans wear a thick moral coat of virtue on political freedom issues. They have earned the right to criticize those who do not live up to American standards.

Not long after Guantanamo was established, I met one of China's most thoughtful young intellectuals. We discussed Guantanamo. He said that it had had a profound impact on Chinese intellectuals. Before Guantanamo, they had accepted the right of Americans to stand on a moral pedestal and lecture China on human rights issues. After Guantanamo, the pedestal had vanished. This young Chinese said to me with masterful understatement: "We Chinese have discovered that Americans are not really different from us. We thought they were special. Now we know that they are just like us."

The worst part about Guantanamo, however, is that it might be only the tip of the iceberg. The U.S. government announced the creation of a prison at Guantanamo. It is a regularly debated topic. Many other alleged prisons around the world have not been recognized. As one writer noted, "The Bush administration has still not answered charges leveled in *The Washington Post* which, citing numerous unnamed U.S. officials, described the rendition of captured Al-Qaeda suspects from U.S. custody to other countries, such as Uzbekistan, Pakistan, Egypt, Jordan, Saudi Arabia and Morocco, where they were tortured or mistreated. These countries, like Syria, are ones where the United States itself has criticized the practice of torture."[4]

The moral standing of America in the eyes of the rest of the world is an important determinant of how both America and American power will be perceived by the rest of the world. An America committed to certain values and standards in its behavior will naturally be perceived to be less threatening. An America that is perceived to be playing rough and ready with the rules will naturally be less welcomed. The "legitimacy" of American power is important. The more legitimate it is perceived to be, the more easily it will be accepted. Guantanamo has made a serious dent to this legitimacy.

Another vivid indication of how negative the perception of American power has become can be seen in the transformation of American embassies overseas, from being symbols of an open society to literal fortresses. As a young man growing up in Singapore, I often walked into the United States Information Section (USIS) of the American embassy to enjoy the library. The embassy had only one security guard. Singaporeans could walk freely in and out of the building that housed the American embassy at a time, the 1960s, when Southeast Asia was in turmoil and the Vietnam War was picking up steam. The domestic Communist insurgencies had also not been fully suppressed. In the midst of all this turbulence that America was directly involved in, American diplomats could safely walk the streets and live and work in buildings that were not fortified. Today, virtually all new American embassies are built to resemble fortresses. Previously, American embassies looked welcoming. Their physical openness reflected America's role in the world: they served as symbols of an open society. Today, American embassies look like citadels on the hill, besieged by their own defenses, not open or welcoming. Tom Friedman, in his December 21, 2003, article "Where Birds Don't Fly," recounted this story from a Turkish industrialist: "I was just on a tour to Amman and we stopped our tourist van in front of the U.S. Embassy there. We asked the guide why they need all these tanks around it, and the guy told us that within this American Embassy they have everything they need so they can survive without going outside . . . I felt really sorry for the Americans there."

A cynic might suggest that it is not surprising that American embassies, which are actually supposed to represent the best features of their society, represent symbolically the military power of America. Indeed, American military power is the most visible and in some ways the clearest indication of how much American power dominates the globe. The American population of 290 million is less than 5 percent of the world's population of 6.3 billion. Yet this 5 percent of the world spends today about 50 percent of the world's defense expenditures. This statistic (if some historian could actually verify it) could possibly make America the most militarized nation in history.

I have experienced at first hand the awesome military power of America. I have landed at sea not on one but on two American aircraft carriers, once in the morning and the second in the evening. One of the certificates that I display proudly in my home next to my academic diplomas is a certificate from a U.S. aircraft carrier that gave me the "Order of the Hook" for landing on it on May 6, 1997. I spent the night on the carrier, before flying home the next day. At midnight, while the aircraft carrier was traveling at full speed, two large oil tankers appeared and sailed parallel to the carrier. Lines were shot across. Gasoline tubes were returned on the lines and while the carrier continued at full speed, the refueling carried on all night. Before that, we had witnessed the jets landing and taking off in the dark in practice runs. It was an awesome experience, fully symbolizing how powerful American military power is.

Today, American aircraft carriers dominate all the oceans. Indeed, each aircraft carrier fleet can on its own deploy more firepower than and probably defeat any other nation's military, with the possible exception of the other nuclear powers. Twelve such fleets are deployed around the world everywhere from Norfolk to Yokosuka to the Persian Gulf, and those only make up a portion of American military power.

In theory, American military power should be the most fearsome aspect of American power. In fact, American military power may be the least resented dimension of American power. The American navy today calls on virtually every major port in the world. Their ships rarely meet with protests. The reasons why American military power is not strongly resented are complex.

Probably the most important reason is the global awareness that America, unlike previous military powers, uses its military power sparingly. With all the power it has, America could easily conquer several nations. But in a major departure from European traditions, America decided early on that the use of force to occupy nations was not a trait that it wished to acquire. Instead, at the end of World War II, when America was at one of its peaks of military power, it wove into the U.N. Charter the principles that should legitimize the use of force. Hence, under the international law promoted by America in 1945, the use of force is deemed to be justifiable only under two conditions: if it is exercised in self-defense against an invading force and if it is authorized by the U.N. Security Council. It was because of these prevailing principles that Tony Blair, the British prime minister, worked so hard to persuade President George W. Bush to seek the authorization of the Security Council before intervening militarily in Iraq. One reason why the rest of the world was in some ways astonished and taken aback by the decision of America to go to war after having *failed* to secure a legitimizing Security Council resolution was because of the realization that America had violated the principles that it had embedded into international law at the end of World War II. This lack of explicit legal legitimacy for the Iraq war of 2004 was particularly damaging in the Islamic world because it reinforced the view of many Muslims that military force is used more readily against Muslim citizens, often innocent Muslim citizens. From the downing of a civilian Iranian airliner by an U.S. Air Force jet to the bombing of a Sudanese pharmaceutical factory, from the high-altitude bombing of Afghanistan to the military invasion of Iraq, all these events make some Muslims believe that their lives matter less when U.S. military force is deployed.

Despite this, the Iraq war still remains an aberration. It has demonstrated how rarely American military power is used. The one area where American checks and balances do seem to work overseas are the checks and balances on use of military power. These checks and balances only work because the use of American military power is both visible and expensive. The voters and taxpayers have to be brought along. Covert military operations, before 9/11, were rare. The public is kept fully informed when the military goes into action. Each casualty is reported immediately and daily, even though this could have a corrosive effect on the political support for such operations and indeed endanger the reelection of politicians and leaders. Since all politicians know that they put their own political careers on the line when they authorize or launch American military operations, they have a vested interest in being cautious about using American military power. This is why Israel is wise not to rely on American soldiers to defend it. The American people are ready to provide economic, financial, and political support to a state that they believe to be beleaguered. But if American servicemen were seen to be dying in defense of Israel, a pullout could easily occur, despite the extremely close ties between America and Israel.

Domestic constraints are not the only reasons American military power is respected overseas. Few nations believe that they face the threat of an American military invasion. Possibly not even Castro. The paradox of Castro is that on the one hand the force that works most against him is American power. Yet, his ability to survive despite the pressures of this enormous force has in turn transformed him into a global political giant. Without American pressures, he would have the same status as any other political leader. America has made Castro politically significant.

More importantly, American military power is welcomed in many parts of the world because its presence is more often stabilizing rather than destabilizing. The region that illustrates this best is East Asia. The East Asian economic miracle of the 1980s and 1990s had to rest on a stable political platform. This stable political platform was based to some extent on the strong American military presence. Conceivably millions of lives and billions of dollars have been saved by this military presence.

Northeast Asia is potentially one of the most dangerous areas of the world. The Korean Peninsula is divided. The Demilitarized Zone (DMZ) that separates the two Koreas has two of the most powerful military forces facing each other, with enormous capacity to wreak destruction upon each other. Thirty-seven thousand American troops are on the frontline here. They have been there for over half a century. The Korean Peninsula is in turn located in a tight political corner between Japan and China. A huge residue of suspicions exists in the relationships between North Korea, China, and Japan, although the North Korean-Chinese relationship is the least problematic. Japan has every reason to feel insecure in this neighborhood. Without American protection it would have heavily rearmed itself. Indeed, given its enormous economic power, it would have been quite natural for Japan to have gone nuclear, which could have in turn triggered a fierce regional nuclear competition. The fear of a new nuclear arms race is still alive today: "Experts talk of wide repercussions—of an atomic Iran inspiring nuclear ambitions in other Middle Eastern countries, and of North Korea prompting rapid proliferation in the Far East."[5]

The main reason why Japan has not gone nuclear is because of the American military presence, which has stabilized the geopolitical environment around Japan and provided Japan far greater security than Japan could have provided for itself militarily. In keeping Japan non-nuclear, America has also done a favor to all of Japan's neighbors: Russia, Korea, and China. All of these countries know that the American military presence can be stabilizing, not disruptive. It has helped to preserve a balance of power. The American military presence in East Asia is among the most formidable of any American deployment in the world. But America has never felt any real political pressure from the region to remove it or reduce it (with the possible exception of Okinawa). The Philippines, in one of its nationalist moments, evicted the American military from its bases in Clark and Subic, but many Filipinos privately regret this eviction now.

In doing Japan and its neighbors a favor, America has also helped itself. The Japanese have formidable technological skills. In the field of manufacturing, Japan has clearly demonstrated that it can be number one. If Japan had decided to go nuclear, it is not inconceivable that Japan could have the world's most technologically sophisticated nuclear weaponry, certainly far more sophisticated than Soviet or Russian nuclear weaponry. America in turn would be caught in a nuclear arms race with Japan because, for its own security, it would not have allowed another nation to have more sophisticated nuclear capability. China would then have felt compelled to keep up with Japan. This would in turn first have pulled India to increase its nuclear arsenal to keep up with China. Pakistan would then have had no obvious choice but to keep pace with India. The huge American military presence in East Asia has not just been a gift to the region. It has also been a gift to American security.

There are other forces that have restrained Japan from going nuclear (and it is widely believed that Japan could almost immediately transform itself into a nuclear power, as it has perfected all the key components of a nuclear weapons program, from rocketry to developing nuclear fuel rods.) In fact, Japan has the third largest number of active nuclear reactors in the world, behind the United States and France. Japanese guilt from World War II has not been fully erased.

The Japanese body politic is still reluctant to support aggressive nationalist politicians, even though the trend is in their favor.

Probably one of the biggest restraining factors on Japan (and other major nations) going nuclear was the norms that America created against the proliferation of nuclear weapons. These norms are embedded in various U.N. resolutions and international treaties like the Non-Proliferation Treaty (NPT). These norms could have cracked as new powers emerged but they have essentially held (even though many middle powers, such as Brazil, Argentina, Iran, and Egypt, privately regret foregoing the nuclear option). The tragedy here is that the one country that developed these norms, America, may actually be endangering these norms by walking away from treaties that have helped to sustain them, including the Comprehensive Test Ban Treaty (CTBT) and Anti-Ballistic Missile Treaty (ABMT). Consistency of American behavior is so important to the world precisely because so many norms rest upon American leadership in preserving them.

America has also set benign rules of the game in many other areas. The last sixty years of world history have seen among the most explosive growth of merchandise and people flows all across the world. Global trade continues to grow steadily. Many reasons explain this: technology, open markets (an ideology spread by American influence), political stability, global trading rules (another American legacy). But one important factor that is rarely mentioned or recognized is the spread of American military power around the world. American military power keeps global sea and air routes open. Any force that tries to disrupt these routes will have to reckon with America. Since no country can, global trade has flourished. There are many narrow straits that are traversed by major international sea routes. The Law of the Sea Convention declares that these straits should be kept open. But if any littoral state were to be tempted to close them, they would have to contend with the American navy. Even Canada discovered that it could not close its waters near the North Pole when the American navy decided to sail through them. A strong American navy helps the world.

Indeed, it is hardly an exaggeration to say that all the global trading powers are essentially free riding on the American military presence. They benefit enormously and directly from the global American military presence, which costs American taxpayers over $400 billion a year. But other nations pay not a penny for this. America has been remarkably generous in providing such a service to the globe (and this makes it all the more puzzling that America frets so much about its annual contribution to the U.N. regular and peacekeeping budgets, which only cost about $1 billion a year, or 1/400th of its defense expenditure).

The strange paradox here is that American military power, which is probably the strongest military force in human history, has sat very lightly on the world, indeed benefited it. By contrast, American political and economic power, which is largely invisible to the naked eye, has sat heavily on the world and significantly altered the destinies of nations and continents. Probably every society on earth has in one way or another been directly or indirectly affected by American political and economic power. The ones that were affected most deeply still carry scars that influence their attitudes towards America today.

Many of the interventions that America made in other societies, directly or indirectly, were often dictated by Cold War considerations, when America and the Soviet Union were both playing a zero-sum game of winning or losing nations. Perhaps if there had been no Cold War, America may not have intervened in Africa or the Islamic world (although its heavy hand in Latin America predated the Cold War). It is also true that many of these nations were not hapless victims. Their ruling elites often skillfully played one power off against another. American policymakers probably believed then that they were only playing by the rules of the day in the Cold War era but they altered the history of many nations.

American political and economic power arrives subtly, perhaps subversively. Rarely can it be captured or displayed on TV screens. Yet, American political and economic power has the capacity to transform countries completely, affecting the daily lives of millions of their citizens. When this happens, very few Americans are aware of it.

The net effect of American involvement in shaping the political and economic destinies of nations has meant that America has made a deep impression on many societies around the globe. After the Cold War ended, America believed that it could walk away from this history. The nations that were affected could not.

It would be impossible in a slim volume like this to do an ency-clopedic survey. This brief chapter can only provide brief sketches on how American political and economic power has influenced the world. No region has been left untouched.

Latin America has a unique relationship with America. It also provides probably the best living laboratory to study the real im-pact of American power. If American power has had a fundamen-tally benign impact on other societies, the region most likely to have experienced such benign effects should have been Latin America. Since the enunciation of the Monroe Doctrine in 1823, there has been no doubt that America has had both a strong interest and in-volvement in the political and economic fortunes of Latin America. For most of the twentieth century, Latin America served as the strategic backyard of the United States. But while most Americans tend the backyards of their homes well, considering them an inte-gral part of their personal space, America as a country does not seem to have done a good job of tending its strategic backyard.

When the twentieth century opened, America showed great promise. A historian looking ahead then would have also predicted an equally good century ahead for Latin America. Argentina, for example, was one of the wealthiest countries of the world when the century opened. Culturally, Latin America was closely linked to Europe, even though its indigenous cultures had varying degrees of external influence. Buenos Aires had the potential of becoming the Paris or Milan of Latin America. There should have been no fundamental cultural barriers to Latin Americans enjoying the same kind of economic growth that America or Europe enjoyed in the twentieth century.

With the American economic engine experiencing explosive growth in the twentieth century, the first countries that could have and should have hitched their wagons to this rapidly accelerating locomotive should have been Latin American. Even if they did not grow as rapidly, they should have at least found themselves better off at the end of the century than the beginning. Instead, the twentieth century has been a wasted century for many Latin American nations. Argentina went from having the thirteenth highest per capita GDP in 1900 to the sixty-ninth highest today.

If America had begun exporting its values to Latin America at the beginning of the twentieth century, there should have been a thriving community of peaceful and prosperous democracies by the end of the century, a community similar to that found in Western Europe. Instead, by the end of the century, while there had been a proliferation of democracies at the end of the Cold War (when America no longer had a vested interest in keeping right-wing dictators in office to prevent Soviet influence from coming in), few Latin American societies were experiencing real peace and prosperity. "In the last few years, six elected heads of state have been ousted in the face of violent unrest, something nearly unheard of in the previous decade. A widely noted United Nations survey of 19,000 Latin Americans in 18 countries in April produced a startling result: a majority would choose a dictator over an elected leader if that provided economic benefits."[6] This longing for economic success combined with a very slim amount of patience for new leaders has produced a frustrated region that is both angry and disillusioned with America.

What America is reaping in Latin America at the end of the twentieth century is the result of the seeds it has sown in its strategic backyard throughout the century. The problem here is that American policymakers have never tried to honestly analyze the impact of their policies in Latin America.

In November 2003, I attended in New York a special celebration of the writings of the Nobel Laureate Gabriel García Marquez. The evening, brilliant and spectacular, was organized by PEN, the authors' association. Many famous writers came personally to the theater to honor Marquez. We also watched a video recording of Bill Clinton paying his tribute to the writer. As the evening wore on, one could feel a warm sense of solidarity. The evening seemed to suggest that there was a spiritual harmony between America and Latin America, between two peoples celebrating the same values.

This evening ended with a message sent to this celebratory occasion by Marquez himself. In it he explained why he had refused to come to America personally to receive the accolades paid to him that evening. His message that night was similar to that contained in his letter to President Bush on 9/11: "How does it feel now that horror is erupting in your own yard and not in your neighbor's living room? . . . Do you know that between 1824 and 1994 your country carried out 73 invasions in countries of Latin America? . . . For almost a century, your country has been at war with the entire world. . . . How does it feel, Yank, knowing that on September 11th the long war finally reached your home?"

Good writers capture the soul of their societies. Gabriel García Marquez lives in Colombia, one of the most troubled countries on the continent. But the message that he conveyed that night and in that letter could have been conveyed by many other Latin Americans. To Marquez, America was not a society that was a beacon of hope to Latin America. Instead it was a society that had sat oppressively upon Latin America and only strengthened, not weakened, the many maladies of Latin America.

The curious thing about Latin America is that it has been hurt by virtually all American policies, even after these policies have been reversed. During the Cold War, in an effort to keep Soviet influence out, America was closely allied with military dictatorships all over Latin America, including in the biggest societies of Brazil, Argentina, and Chile. When the Cold War ended, America exported democracy. The region was initially exuberant when these military dictators were removed. A decade of democracy followed. But, with the exception of Chile, none of the Latin American societies seem better off. In 1991, at the height of the post–Cold War love affair between America and Latin America, the Argentine government under President Carlos Menem actually announced that Argentina would have "carnal relations" with America. Argentina withdrew from the Non-Aligned Movement and declared that it would become an ally of America. In the early 1990s, Argentina was held up as a "star pupil" of the "Washington consensus" and the IMF. The Argentine finance minister, Domingo Cavallo, was also held up as a role model for the world. Argentina's future looked buoyant. Within a decade, Argentina had crashed and burned. It was given no special helping hand from America. Instead it was made to accept bitter economic medicine from the IMF, which put the social and political stability of Argentina under great stress.

The story of America and Argentina should ordinarily concern only two countries. It should be of no consequence to the rest of the world. But in the small globalized world that we live in, the soured love affair of America and Argentina was watched intensely. If the result had been a happy one, many other countries would have followed suit. And America would have had a string of suitors queuing up to get closer to it. Instead the relationship crashed, and the potential suitors dispersed.

Of course Argentina had homegrown flaws. Like many Latin American nations, many elements of its social structure remain feudal. Wealth and land ownership are still concentrated in the hands of a few well-established families. There is little or no social mobility of the kind that is flourishing in America. It will be difficult for any Latin American society to produce a Bill Gates, because the barriers to movement across social classes are formidable. The Latin Americans cannot hold America responsible for their own failure to release themselves from the clutches of feudalism. But they can legitimately ask whether the introduction of American power into their region has had a beneficial or negative effect.

The most successful country in Latin America today in both political and economic terms is probably Chile. It is also now the most stable Latin American country. It provides an interesting case study of how American power has influenced the development of other states and how this history continues to be "alive" in these countries.

In early 2003 when America approached the Chilean Government to vote in favor of a resolution in the U.N. Security Council to legitimize the American intervention in Iraq, virtually the entire Chilean society rebelled at the thought. The leftist political forces in Chile opposed American intervention in any other country because they remembered vividly the trauma that Chilean society went through when the CIA engineered the removal of President Allende in 1973. The rightist political forces in Chile opposed American intervention because they remembered the trauma Chile went through when the United States encouraged the removal of General Pinochet in 1990. Politically, the left and the right in Chile disagree on almost everything. But they agreed completely on one thing: American intervention to change the political course of any society is wrong. The recent history of Chile (or perhaps of Latin America) has convinced them of this.

In the months of February and March 2003 the Chilean government was put under enormous pressure from the American government to relent in its opposition to the war in Iraq and to vote in favor of the American resolution in the Security Council. There were hints that the newly proposed Free Trade Agreement might be jeopardized.

The refusal of the Chilean government and society to buckle under this enormous pressure made heroes out of Chileans in the U.N. community. There was deep concern that Chile would pay a heavy political price with America for keeping to its principles. But wiser counsels prevailed in Washington. The FTA between America and Chile was signed in September 2003, barely four months after the Iraq war. Still, Chile had to pay a small political price. Its ambassador to the United Nations, Ambassador Juan Gabriel Valdés, was transferred to another posting, partly as a symbolic gesture to appease America. He was replaced by an equally distinguished Chilean diplomat, Heraldo Muñoz Ledo, who had had the good fortune of doing his doctorate in international studies at the University of Denver at the same time as the national security adviser, Condoleezza Rice. For the rest of its term on the U.N. Security Council, Chile made every effort not to unnecessarily antagonize America. Indeed, today virtually no nation wants to antagonize America, even if its history may incline it in that direction.

Africa is probably the weakest continent on earth. It lags behind the rest of the world in development and in political and economic stability or growth. It has the largest number of "least developed countries" (a U.N. category to describe some of the poorest states of the world). But it is also far from America and, apart from the painful chapter of slavery, there have been no deep historical contacts between America and Africa. If Americans are asked to describe the impact of American power on Africa, they would say that American policy towards Africa is at best one of benign neglect. This is partially true. Many Africans would probably like America to do more for them. But there is no will in the American body politic to do this.

The phrase "benign neglect," however, does not accurately describe the impact of American power on Africa. In Africa, the main decisions that affect its political and economic evolutions are made not on the continent itself but in Washington, D.C. (and partly in some key European capitals like Paris and London).

Two nations living side by side in West Africa, Liberia and Sierra Leone, illustrate how decisions made in Washington and London can influence the fate of African nations. Liberia is America's godchild in Africa. It was a nation founded by and for the freed American slaves returning to Africa. It was always an artificial state that survived by maintaining a special relationship with America. Its currency for a long time was the American dollar. Psychologically, Liberians felt that they were America's children in Africa. Despite this closeness to America, Liberia suffered the kind of political collapse common in the Third World: misrule by a corrupt family, the Tubmans. The Tubman era ended in 1971 with the death of President William V. S. Tubman. In 1980, following an interim period of rule by William R. Tolbert Jr., Tubman's vice president, a brutal sergeant named Samuel K. Doe staged a coup, executing Tolbert. He committed numerous atrocities but as this was during the Cold War, America condoned Sergeant Doe and provided his government $500 million dollars in assistance. A *New York Times* correspondent, Bill Berkeley, documented this relationship in his book, *The Graves Are Not Yet Full: Race, Tribe, and Power in the Heart of Africa.*

When the Cold War ended, Liberia's travails did not. It suffered disaster after disaster, ending with the "democratic" election of

Charles Taylor in 1997. Taylor too was a notoriously brutal and corrupt ruler. He would have been ignored by the rest of the world if he had stuck to misrule in his own country. Instead he foolishly decided to support the brutal "Revolutionary United Front" (RUF) of Sierra Leone, which became infamous because of its horrendous strategy of cutting off the hands of all its victims. RUF quickly become recognized as a force as evil as the Khmer Rouge or the Taleban.

Both Liberia and Sierra Leone could have been left to drift into decades of misrule, with little international intervention. But in 2000, the RUF made the mistake of taking U.N. peacekeeping officers hostage. The RUF forces also appeared to be on the verge of taking over the capital of Sierra Leone, Freetown. In attempting this, both Charles Taylor and the RUF had dangerously overreached themselves. Security Council members became aware that the credibility of the council would be damaged if RUF was not rebuffed. More importantly, Tony Blair's father had once taught at Fourah Bay College in Freetown, Sierra Leone. Tony Blair therefore took an unusually close personal interest in the Sierra Leone situation. He dispatched a strong British military force to save Freetown and gradually push back the RUF forces.

Sierra Leone was saved only because it happened to have powerful friends in London who viewed sympathetically the plight of a former colony. The British invasion of Sierra Leone under Tony Blair's leadership can truly be characterized as a rare act of altruism in international affairs. No significant British interests were enhanced by this intervention. By contrast, Liberia, which was once America's godchild, quickly became America's unwanted stepchild in Africa. There was little appetite in Washington to save it and Liberia, unlike Sierra Leone, had to suffer a few more years before Charles Taylor was eventually removed.

America cannot take responsibility for the continent of Africa. If any continent should, it should be Europe. William Pfaff once asked,

"Who is responsible for the African catastrophe?" and answered, "The European powers who colonized Africa in the nineteenth century out of an immensely complex mixture of good and bad motives, thereby destroying Africa's existing social and political systems, its customary institutions and law." He then asked, "Who outside Africa has an urgent material interest in Africa's salvation?" His answer was, "The Europeans. Besides the fact that Europe is the principal consumer of African mineral and agricultural exports, Africa's foundering means that hundreds of thousands, even millions more desperate people are attempting to get out of Africa to places where they can find order, jobs, security, a future. Their scarcely controllable migration towards Europe already has created immense social problems and serious political tensions."[7]

This would seem to imply that America can walk away from any sense of responsibility for Africa. Many Americans also ask, quite reasonably, why they should be held responsible for the misrule that has plagued so many Third World countries, especially African countries. America did not colonize these countries, Europe did. In any case colonial rule ended decades ago. How can Third World countries continue to blame Europe, let alone America, for their failures?

One answer lies in the American-dominated international institutions whose role is to serve as a safety net to rescue nations in distress. Several institutions were set up after World War II but the two that have had greatest global influence are the United Nations Security Council (UNSC), whose charter responsibility is to respond to "threats to peace and security," and the International Monetary Fund (IMF), one of whose charter responsibilities is to rescue nations in financial distress, arising, for example, from loss of confidence in their currencies by international financial markets.

In theory these two institutions are meant to function like fire departments of a large city. When a fire breaks out in New York City, for example, the fire department rushes to put it out, regardless of whether it breaks out in the wealthy Park Avenue area or in the poorer Bronx or Harlem areas. There is no discrimination on the basis of wealth or power. The Security Council and the IMF, however, function like fire departments that only respond to distress calls when the flames flicker at the edges of rich and powerful neighborhoods. If the rich are not affected, the poor are abandoned and left to burn in conflict or in financial distress.

Since America is the most powerful member of the international community (and consequently is in effect in control of the major decisions of the Security Council and the IMF), it also holds the fate of many weaker countries in its hands. Many Americans believe that the Security Council is *not* under American control, as evidenced by the recent refusal of the UNSC to endorse the war in Iraq. It is true that the Security Council can from time to time resist American efforts to secure support or endorsement, as in the war in Iraq or earlier in the refusal to endorse the American-led NATO campaign in Kosovo. It is true that America does not have absolute power to make the Security Council act when it does not want to. But it is also true that America has absolute power to block the UNSC from acting in response to certain crises. Sadly, such American decisions to block the Security Council from acting have resulted in severe loss of life. America's decisions in the Security Council have life-and-death consequences elsewhere on the globe.

East Asia also illustrates how decisions made in Washington by a few key people can rescue millions from poverty, or they can throw millions into deeper poverty. One consequence of the Asian financial crisis on Indonesia was that over 50 million people fell back into poverty. The people who live at the very bottom of the economic system across the globe fall into poverty with no one noticing, until it spills over into political unrest or conflict, creating safe havens for terrorists. Terrorists like to swim in such seas of discontent as they provide them with the best protection and the best recruiting grounds. Even now, more than seven years after the financial crisis first rocked Indonesia, the full story of the miseries that the Indonesian people experienced in this crisis has not been fully documented. Nor have there been any proper studies of how crucial decisions made in Washington may have aggravated, rather than ameliorated, this crisis.

Many Americans with whom I have discussed the role of American decisionmakers in the Indonesian financial crisis, have a natural inclination to ask: "But who was responsible for these policies? Why have they not been held accountable for their actions?" Such questions miss the point. The real story is a much more complex one, both in political and moral terms. I happen to know many of the key American policymakers who were involved in these decisions. Some of them are good friends of mine: They are all good, honest, hardworking, and dedicated individuals who believed that they were doing the right thing, both for America and for themselves. There were no evil or irresponsible people involved in any of these major decisions that affected millions of people. Nor were any of them trying deliberately to inflict pain or suffering. The problems are not the result of any rogue policymakers. Indeed the hunt for scapegoats would be most unwise. The problems arising from the impact of American power cannot and will not be addressed until their root causes are dealt with.

The "root causes" of the problem of American power vis-à-vis the rest of the world is that this huge edifice of American power is structurally designed to serve only one purpose: to further American interests. This structural design in turn cannot be easily changed because it is firmly rooted in the American democratic system. The structure of American democracy is functionally designed to produce American leaders and politicians who are elected because they promise to further American interests. Any leader or politician who makes a habit of sacrificing American interests in the favor of other nations' or even global interests will have a very short shelf life. There can be and often is within America a great debate of what exactly American interests are. But there is no debate on whether American interests should ever be put aside in favor of anyone else's.

When responsible American politicians and leaders carry or use this power overseas, they generally have no desire to hurt other countries and they often believe that they are doing the "right thing." Even if U.S. foreign policy sometimes leads to unfortunate results, policymakers invariably believe that this was not the result of any malevolent intentions. It is almost as if the consequences don't matter if the intentions are good. That might play well with the domestic U.S. electorate, but those consequences matter viscerally abroad.

Hence the American response to the Asian financial crisis in Indonesia in 1996–98 was revealing. The consequences of American policies were often ruinous, even though all the U.S. policymakers acted in the belief they were helping Indonesia. To understand the difficulties of comprehending what really happened, you have to assemble three documents and read them side by side. The first is chapter nine of Robert Rubin's memoirs, entitled *In an Uncertain World*. As the American treasury secretary then, Robert Rubin was probably the most important actor in the drama. The second is chapter four of Joseph Stiglitz's famous and controversial book, *Globalization and Its Discontents*. Stiglitz, who was the chief economist of the World Bank during the crisis, also had a ringside view of what happened and could see immediately the results of each action taken. The third document is a front-page article in the *Wall Street Journal*, the seventh in a series on American power and the world. The three offer distinctively different points of view of the same American intervention to help Indonesia in crisis.

Rubin characterized the Indonesian crisis as a struggle between the corrupt government of President Suharto and the international financial markets, which had suddenly lost confidence in Indonesia. The rupiah plunged. Social unrest grew. When alerted to this crisis, representatives of both the IMF and the Treasury came to Indonesia as "white knights," trying hard to come up with plans and resources to stabilize the Indonesian economy. Alas, the plan failed when Suharto's corrupt government ignored the IMF plans and tried instead to protect the corrupt cronies and the members of Suharto's family. If only Suharto had complied with these IMF plans, all would have been well. The good guys were the Americans and the IMF and the bad guys were the corrupt Indonesian officials.

Sadly, Rubin failed to mention the disastrous effects of statements made by senior Treasury officials during the crisis. At one point, Deputy Secretary Larry Summers issued a statement signaling Washington's support for strong IMF measures. The immediate effect was to cause a run on the rupiah. There was a real danger that riots could have broken out all over the country as a result of this statement. Fortunately, diplomatic intervention overnight led to Summers qualifying his statement, which in turn calmed the social and political situation in Indonesia. Clearly, America does not need an aircraft carrier to destabilize a country. A single statement by a senior Treasury official at a time of crisis can throw an entire country off balance. (Something similar happened in late July 2002 when Paul O'Neill, then treasury secretary, made some remarks that caused a run on the Brazilian currency.)

Nor does Rubin mention, except in passing, a debate that also took place in Washington, D.C., at that time as to whether America was better off supporting the continuation of Suharto's government or allowing (or encouraging) it to fall. Twenty-five years from now, when the records are finally released, we will understand the terms of the debate. Was the question asked: Would the fall of Suharto be good for American interests? Rubin did say in his book, "Jim Steinberg of the NSC said in one of our meetings that perhaps we should be reaching out to the reform forces in Indonesia, so that if Suharto did fall, they wouldn't feel we'd been their opponents."[8] This was wise advice for protecting American interests. But were Indonesian interests also factored in these discussions in Washington?

Joseph Stiglitz offered a very different view of what happened. As he said, "When the crisis broke out, I was surprised at how strongly the IMF and the U.S. Treasury seemed to criticize the countries—according to the IMF, the Asian nations' institutions were rotten, their governments corrupt, and wholesale reform was needed."[9] But Stiglitz noted that these were the same governments that the World Bank had only a year or two earlier decided were responsible for "The East Asian Miracle." How could the same governments be responsible for both the miracle and the meltdown?

Stiglitz wrote that "the IMF now agrees it made serious mistakes in its fiscal policy advice, in how it pushed bank restructuring in Indonesia, in perhaps pushing capital market liberalization prematurely."[10] The results of their mistakes were enormously costly for the Indonesian population. Poverty doubled. The political system was shaken. Stiglitz's thesis is clear: Indonesia suffered because of policy mistakes made in Washington, not Jakarta. American power drove these decisions.

The third account of the same financial crisis is no less revealing. The *Wall Street Journal* described simply and clinically how at a time when the American government officials were stating that the root cause of the Indonesian crisis was corruption, American government officials in Jakarta were simultaneously instructed to protect "contracts" signed between American companies and the corrupt cronies of Suharto. The *Wall Street Journal* article quoted Edmund McWilliams, who was chief political counselor at the U.S. embassy in Jakarta from 1996 to 1999, as saying that in Indonesia's case, "protecting the interests of major investors and creditors was at the center of the table in everything we did. Concerns about stability made it to the margins. Concerns about human rights, democracy, corruption never made it onto the table at all." The article also noted that

> Washington's discordant signals have left a bitter legacy here. A nation once robustly pro-American has become a bastion of anti-U.S. hostility. In 1999, 75% of Indonesians held a favorable view of the U.S., according to the Pew Research Center. In a poll last year, the figure was just 15%. It's the worst anti-Americanism here in 25 years, says Sidney Jones of the International Crisis Group, a non-profit group that monitors global hot spots. This shift has multiple causes, including the war in Iraq. But among them is a widely held view here that in the aftermath of the Suharto dictatorship—a time of crisis but also.of promise—the U.S. threw its weight behind its business interests to the detriment of Indonesians."

The same article also quoted Alwi Shihab, a former foreign minister, as saying, "It was as if the U.S. condoned corruption, but we were in no position to quarrel with them. A lot of momentum for reform was lost."[11]

The *Wall Street Journal* is not known to be anti-American. But this article, which was carried on page 1 of its February 11, 2004, issue as the seventh article in its series "Power and Peril: America's Supremacy and Its Limits," did a brilliant job of explaining how American power had affected Indonesians during one of its most acute crises and why it has left a bitter legacy in Indonesia.

From these three different accounts, it is possible to begin to assemble the essential story of the Indonesian financial crisis. When the crisis hit Indonesia in mid-1997, America intervened in an effort to help Indonesia. But the results did not help the Indonesian people. Over time, a case could be made that both the nature and scope of American interventions may have made the Indonesian people suffer more, not less. This does not absolve the government of President Suharto of its responsibilities. But since only the IMF had the power to send a signal to the markets, and as the IMF took its direction carefully from the policymakers in Washington, in the end the Indonesian drama that was played out was choreographed not by decisions made in Indonesia but by decisions made in Washington. One truth cannot be denied. Washington would never contemplate implementing policies that could trigger the same degree of social and political unrest in North America. Mexico is protected by its proximity to America. Whenever a financial crisis breaks out in Mexico, the entire American government, including the Federal Reserve Bank, swings into action to put the crisis under control.

A starkly different strategy was also adopted when America faced the prospect of a domestic financial crisis that could have done as much damage to the U.S. economy as the Indonesian crisis did to Indonesia. Then the *consequences*, rather than the *causes*, of the crisis became the priority. Hence, Washington organized a massive bailout of the out-of-control hedge fund Long Term Capital Management (LTCM) in fall 1998 to prevent a billion-dollar meltdown in America's banking system. Many intelligent eyes across the world noticed the discrepancy between how America handled a financial crisis close to home and how it handled one far from home. In the former, it worried about the consequences of its action. In the latter, it did not. In an increasingly shrinking world, when the number of pairs of intelligent and well-informed eyes is growing by leaps and bounds, such discrepancies become both clear and magnified. Most sophisticated observers would say that these are only the "realities" of power. The awareness of these "realities" is, however, spreading more widely, which in turn raises the level of global resentment towards American power.

The strongest region in the world, outside America, is Europe. In terms of level of development, wealth accumulation, social capital, and political and economic strength, Europe seems to match North America in almost every area, except military power. There it is a distant second. Europe should therefore be relaxed about the use or abuse of American power. Yet in the years 2001 to 2004, the one region that became the most exercised over the American interventions in Iraq was Europe. Pro-American sentiments dived sharply. A poll conducted by the Pew Research Center from February 19 to March 2004 found that a majority of people interviewed in France and Germany believed that the Iraq war had undermined the struggle against terrorists and doubted the Bush administration's sincerity in trying to combat terror. After the survey, Andrew Kohut, the director of the Pew Center, commented, "We do know that support has been flagging and more Germans and French think we're exaggerating this thing. I think this reflects a general disenchantment with America."[12] Between summer 2002 and spring 2003, U.S. favorability ratings plummeted from 75 percent to 48 percent in Britain, 63 percent to 31 percent in France, and 61 percent to 25 percent in Germany.[13] Even in the countries where the governments strongly supported the war (like the United Kingdom, Italy, and Spain), the populations were clearly opposed to the American intervention in Iraq.

Much has been written about the sudden turnaround in European attitudes towards America. Part of the strong European reactions may be due to their sense of betrayal over America walking away from the norms on the use of force that America and Europe had built jointly after the war. Under the U.N. Charter, a nation could legitimately use force only under two circumstances: as an act of self-defense or if authorized by the U.N. Security Council.

Hence, when America went to war after failing to get Security Council authorization, Europe felt that America had walked away from an edifice of principles that they had jointly built after World War II to "save succeeding generations from the scourge of war, which twice in our lifetime has brought untold sorrow to mankind" (U.N. Charter).

Disagreement over principles seldom explains sharp differences. Different interests are often part of the explanation. America is not situated geographically next to the Islamic world. Europe is. The Islamic populations within Europe are growing. But the Islamic population surrounding Europe is growing even faster. These are the statistics (see figure 1 on page 212). Joel E. Cohen, in his article entitled "Human Population: The Next Half Century," discussed some implications of this difference in population growth: "The projected difference in age structures between the European Union versus North Africa and western Asia has obvious implications for the supplies of military personnel and ratios of elderly to middle-aged."[14]

When the temperature in the Islamic world goes up, Europeans do not just read about it in the newspapers, as some Americans do. They feel the heat on their faces. This is another reason why the Europeans were so upset about America going to war in Iraq without building up a solid international consensus and getting the endorsement of the U.N. Security Council (as America did in the Gulf War). They knew that such a war would stoke Muslim anger.

The European assessment of the reactions of the Islamic populations was not wrong. In August 2002, seven months before the war in Iraq, I toured China as part of a U.N. group of families invited by the Chinese government. We visited Xian, an ancient Chinese city, now famous for its terra cotta warriors. In Xian, we visited an ancient mosque, first established in 742 A.D. during the Tang Dynasty. We were graciously welcomed and taken around by the imam. What made this imam unusual was that he was ethnically and culturally

Han Chinese (not Arab, Turkic, or Iranian). He spoke in Mandarin to our group. At the end of the tour, just as we were leaving after a warm and hospitable visit, he turned to us and said that he had only one request to make on our return to New York. He said: "Please tell America not to go to war in Iraq."

Xian is culturally as far away from the Islamic heartland in Saudi Arabia as Norway or South Africa is. To meet a Chinese imam who was so deeply concerned about the impending war in Iraq was a clear signal that the sentiment against the war was both wide and deep in the Islamic world. America did not recognize it. Europe did. Europe also felt that America was directly threatening European interests in going to war. But for all the strength of Europe it could do nothing to stop the war. Such is the nature of American power. No force today can stop it.

From Latin America to Africa, from East Asia to the Islamic world, and even in Europe, there is no region in the world that is immune to the effects of American power. It is the single most important force operating globally, affecting daily the destinies of all nations. But this is a force that has not yet been properly understood or explained in a comprehensive fashion.

Scholars who try to understand all the dimensions of American power are in some ways like the three blind men who try to describe an elephant by feeling different parts. They can only describe the different parts they feel but they cannot portray the animal as a whole.

Many people living outside America believe that a single pair of hands, or a few pairs of hands, is guiding the flow of this American power. They assume that the decisionmakers in Washington are aware of the impact of their decisions. In fact, many American policymakers are unaware of the enormous power that they possess. One of the key reasons for the growing divide between America and the rest of the world is that Americans are generally unaware of the impact of their power while the rest of the world is acutely aware of it.

American power is not guided by a comprehensive or coherent policy designed to shape the world in a certain direction. The founding fathers of America were geniuses in ensuring that no single pair of hands would ever get hold of all the levers of American power. Checks and balances ensured that power was spread throughout the government. The founding fathers also put the ultimate power of the republic in the hands of its citizens. Americans can vote out any leader or party that has abused the powers vested in them by the American constitution. If the American electorate believes their government is not doing its job or representing their interests, they have the ability to correct its course through the ballot box. American voters can reassure themselves every four years that the government they have is their government.

The other 6 billion citizens who are also affected strongly, perhaps even more strongly, by decisions made in Washington have no means of influencing the American decisionmaking process except by appealing to American self-interest (and occasionally American principles). The stronger countries can occasionally temper some of the effects of the American power. The weaker countries cannot.

American power, which was always intended as a force for good, could therefore, paradoxically, become the single most significant cause of turbulence in the twenty-first century. This will happen not because Americans want or desire this. Indeed it may even happen even though most Americans do not want it to. When American power flows overseas it is beyond the control of any individual. The only way to affect its flow is to develop a comprehensive understanding of how it works. It is vital to understand how certain structural features of American power are going to affect the course of world history. Because it is inevitable that they will.

~ 6 ~

Managing American Power

"WITH GREAT POWER COMES great responsibility." These were the parting words of advice given to Spiderman by his uncle. Virtually all Americans would agree with the spirit of this statement, assuming that if they had great power, they too would exercise it with great responsibility.

But one of the most inescapable conclusions of this book is that the global perception of American irresponsibility is likely to grow, rather than diminish, in the coming decades. The irony here is that this will happen even though the intentions of the American population towards the rest of the world will remain benign. Benign intentions, unhappy consequences. How can this happen?

Two great forces will collide to determine the nature of America's interaction with the rest of the world. The first will be American democracy. America has the best and the strongest democracy in the world. On a day-to-day basis, the American political scene seems chaotic. On any particular day, several political forces are at play to determine American political directions: from the president and the executive branch to Congress, the legislative branch; from the Supreme Court and the extensive judicial system to the independent media. On any day, thousands of voices clamor to be heard. All this contentiousness may give the impression of chaos and instability. But, functioning like a well-engineered system, the elaborate checks and balances do result in the American political system reflecting the wishes of the American population over the long run. Over time, to win the votes of the American people, the American government delivers what the American people want. At any point of time, if the American government needs to choose between meeting the wishes of the 6 billion other people on the planet or the 290 million people in America, there would be no contest. It would heed the wishes of the voters, not the non-voters. Democracy is destiny.

The second great force is globalization. Globalization has shrunk the world. For five thousand years, mankind lived in separate communities, separated by oceans, rivers, and mountain ranges. There would be brief contacts but by and large our destinies were determined by forces within our own communities. Today, the term "global village" has already become a cliché. Sadly, it has become a cliché before we have fully grasped its meaning.

For a start, our world is an unhappy, rather than happy, global village. U.N. Secretary-General Kofi Annan has described it well. If the village had a thousand inhabitants, this is how it would look:

> Some 150 of the inhabitants live in an affluent area of the village, about 780 in poorer districts. Another 70 or so live in a neighborhood that is in transition. The average income per person is $6,000 a year, and there are more middle income families than in the past. But just 200 people dispose of 86 per cent of all the wealth, while nearly half of the villagers are eking out an existence on less than $2 a day. . . .

Still, some 220 villagers—two thirds of them women—are illiterate. Of the 390 inhabitants under 20 years of age, three fourths live in the poorer districts, and many are looking desperately for jobs that do not exist. Fewer than 60 people own a computer and only 24 have access to the Internet. More than half have never made or received a telephone call . . . "[1]

Many societies have lived before with such huge disparities. Over time, the advanced societies have learned how to create social and political stability despite huge disparities in income and wealth. The essential trick was to make even the lower classes stakeholders in stability rather than instability. Living in nineteenth century Britain and witnessing at first-hand the conditions in Britain and in Europe, Karl Marx confidently predicted revolution. But the revolution never came. The ruling elites in Europe wisely staved off the revolution by giving the poor the right to vote in members of Parliament. They also created social safety nets to help the desperately poor. At the same time, the rapidly industrializing economies of Europe were able to offer jobs and better living conditions. The rising economic tide did lift most of the boats.

In the global village that we have developed, we are doing virtually the exact opposite of what the Europeans did to stave off the revolution. Instead of enfranchising the poor of our planet, we are disenfranchising them. Almost all the key decisions that affect their lives are made without their having any vote or say. Nor are there any social safety nets. There are miniscule aid flows from the rich to the poor, but they are driven by political considerations, not humanitarian or long-term considerations.

Most importantly, there is no sense of community in this global village. Each family house works on the principle that it is obliged to take care of its own household, not the wider community. There is a minimal set of rules that govern the open spaces, most of which are skewed in favor of the few rich occupants. More dangerously, most of the decisions that affect the fate of the whole village are made by one incredibly rich and powerful household, the American mansion. Some of these decisions benefit the whole village. Many don't. The American household is blithely ignorant of the consequences of its actions for the rest of the village. It does not take a genius to predict that such conditions will result in a rising tide of resentment.

One remarkable paradox about this global village is that the occupants of the household with the best information resources are among the least well-informed about what happens outside their house. Like many other large societies, America has wrapped itself up in a comfortable insularity. Most American TV stations, radio stations, and print media focus almost entirely on domestic issues. During the infamous Monica Lewinsky episode, American eyes stayed glued to their TV sets. Most Americans assumed that this was an American drama being watched by American eyes. But the American media organizations do not just control the airwaves in America. They also control the airwaves all over the world. CNN (and often Fox, too) is watched in virtually every corner of the world. So too are the *International Herald Tribune* and the *Wall Street Journal* read in most major capitals in the world. The result of all this is that the domestic drama that Americans watch on their TV sets is only a play within a play. When Americans watch Monica Lewinsky, the rest of the world watches the Americans watching Monica Lewinsky. It would be no exaggeration to say that for the rest of the world, Americans have become like goldfish in a bowl, absorbed and self-contained in their little universe with, apparently, little or no awareness of the eyes watching them from outside.

The message sent out daily by this arrangement is one that America never intended to send: that America is indifferent. Because most of the rest of the world can see clearly what is happening in America, they assume in turn that with the same technology American eyes can also "see" the rest of the world. They would be surprised to learn that the rest of the world rarely appears in the American media. Indeed, it is virtually impossible in most American cities, even though often more than a hundred TV channels are fed into living rooms, to get any kind of regular flow of international news. It is a shocking fact that one can be better informed on the state of the world while sitting in a hotel room in Africa than in a hotel room anywhere in America. From extensive personal experience, I can make this claim confidently. For all practical purposes, America could well be on a different planet, so cut off are Americans from flows of information about events outside America.

Further, when American society explodes with some new domestic frenzy, whether it be Watergate or Monicagate, it generates an enormous "noise." Many Americans assume that this "noise" is confined to American shores. But thanks to U.S. dominance of global media, it isn't. When American eyes are focused on the Super Bowl, the rest of the world is indifferent. The rest of the world is more interested in Manchester United than in the New York Giants. American sports are insular. But that doesn't stop the other noise that flows remorselessly into the rest of the world with all the charm of a super-amplified pickup truck.

Hence, the 6 billion other citizens of the planet have to share an ever-shrinking space with a progressively "noisy" neighbor whose domestic affairs are thrust into the faces of the rest of the world. Many of them may be concerned with more urgent and pressing needs. But they turn on their TV sets to find the weird reality television of American domestic life instead. This is dangerous. Most Americans are aware of the image of Nero fiddling while Rome burned. The rest of the world watches Americans fiddling while the world burns, sometimes from bush fires started or fanned by careless American policies.

This is not how Americans want to think of themselves. Most individual Americans want to help their fellow citizens, be they local or global. Most "intend" only to help the world. If America occasionally harms the rest of the world, Americans believe that this can be the result only of "unintended consequences." However, one new law that Americans may have to familiarize themselves with is "the law of *intended* consequences," because this is how the rest of the global village views American actions.

Take the case of U.S. "domestic" cotton subsidies. The intent of subsidies was to help American farmers, not hurt African farmers. If the American farmer lived in a separate village from the African farmer, one would not affect the other. But they now live in the same village. And the subsidies are disastrous for the African farmers. Once, it could have been argued that the American cotton farmers did not "intend" to hurt their African brothers. Now however, the linkage is inescapable. The information has been widely reported in the American media. Ignorance is no longer an excuse.

The *Wall Street Journal* ran a front page story on June 26, 2002, documenting how the life of a poor cotton farmer in Mali, Mody Sangera of Korokiro, was directly affected by the subsidies that went to American farmers like Ken Hood of Gunnison, Mississippi. Each day, Mody Sangera would have to hitch his one-blade plow to his oxen and begin the first of the fourteen days it would take him to till his fifteen acres of cotton. He would be lucky if he made $2,000, from which he had to support two dozen people. By contrast, Ken Hood would step into his air-conditioned tractor and comfortably drive, with the assistance of a global positioning satellite system, through his ten-thousand-acre spread. As a result of generous congressionally determined subsidies, he will make over a million dollars a year. So what links Ken Hood to Mody Sangera? Thanks to massive subsidies, American farmers are assured of seventy cents per pound regardless of the world price of cotton. They are then able to dump the excess cotton that they produce on the world market and depress the world cotton prices. This in turn further impoverishes African farmers like Mody Sangera. America is cheating market forces; Africa is suffering from them.

Americans now have no shortage of information on the damaging global effects of domestic subsidies. On the eve of the World Trade Talks in Cancún, Mexico, in September 2003, the *New York Times,* probably the most influential newspaper in America, ran a series of articles and editorials that comprehensively documented how American subsidies had hurt African farmers. An article published on September 10, 2003, told the heartbreaking story of Erikanger Thumbo, a Ugandan cotton farmer who, following the tradition of his father and grandfather, digs the rich soil of Uganda with a hoe. No tractor or even oxen help him. The same *Times* article pointed out that even though African farmers produce cotton at less than fifty cents a pound and American farmers produce it at over seventy cents a pound, the U.S. government cash subsidies of over $2 billion (*Note:* The difference in calculations between the *Wall Street Journal* and the *New York Times* on the total amount of cotton subsidies reflects the difficulty of getting a complete account of these subsidies) had depressed the world cotton price to below thirty-five cents a pound, even below the cost price of a poor African farmer. One simple truth, which many Americans will find difficult to digest, is that some African poverty is manufactured by American government policies.

Many thoughtful Americans are aware of this and have criticized the American policies that have produced African poverty. But even after the *New York Times* ran a series of fierce editorials under the title of "Harvesting Poverty," documenting how American policies had generated poverty in the Third World, nothing changed. The frustration over American subsidies is not confined to Africa. "Mr. [Marcelo] Lima, a former investment banker who owns a cattle ranch near Campina Verde, in southern Brazil, argues that recent trade developments have hurt Brazil's otherwise prosperous agricultural industry. 'Whenever we invest in research and technology and become more competitive than American farmers,' Mr. Lima, 41, said, 'the United States always slaps new tariffs on our goods or grants fresh subsidies to their farmers.'"[2] The Brazilian government has heard the cries of those hurt by cotton subsidies, and confronted America in the World Trade Organization with the case against such subsidies. The "Harvesting Poverty" series of editorials in the *New York Times* explored this subject extensively: "Brazil's lawyers have mounted a compelling case, as even some Bush administration officials privately concede, that America's subsidies have indeed suppressed global prices and stolen market share from others."[3]

One strongly held assumption in America is that information and ideas do matter. The story of cotton subsidies, so far, disproves this assumption. Despite a rising tide of information on the damage done by cotton subsidies, the subsidies are increasing, not decreasing. Oxfam, which is dedicated to eradicating poverty in the Third World, monitors the trends in agricultural policies. Philip Bloomer, director of advocacy at Oxfam, said, "In Europe, we believe that there is a glacial movement in the right direction. In the United States, there is a fairly rapid movement in the opposite direction."[4]

The nature of American democracy explains why American agricultural policies are headed in the wrong direction in terms of global impact. In the keenly contested American political system, the votes of the farm belt have become important. The political contribution of agribusiness has gone up from $37 million in 1992 to $53 million in 2002. Consequently, as Fred Bergstein, the director of the Institute of International Economics, said in the same *New York Times* article, "Our American subsidy system is a crime, it's a sin, but we'll talk a good game and get away with doing almost nothing until after the presidential election."[5]

One fundamental question that needs to be answered is whether the story of cotton subsidies is the exception to the rule in evaluating the impact of American policies on the world. Or is it the rule? The trend line is clear. More and more domestic American policies will have a global impact. The world is shrinking, pulling other countries closer and closer to America. As the total amount of "space" shrinks, the impact of America on the world will inevitably increase. Going by the adage that every action leads to a reaction, the global response to American policies is also likely to increase.

The impact of shrinking space is even stronger in the field of the global environment. No American would want to live in a village where a house with only 4 percent of the village's population belched out 25 percent of the smoke from its large chimneys, with much of the soot falling on the rest of the village. But this is precisely the relationship between America and the world on global environmental issues. In per-capita terms, the American household is by far the largest polluter on the global village. This simple fact is now known to an increasingly well-informed global audience.

Until recently, there was little real concern about the long-distance effects of American pollution because of the belief that there was a limitless amount of atmosphere which would absorb American pollution. The sky was literally the limit. Eventually, everything would get absorbed and even if the rest of the world caught up with America in per-capita levels of pollution, there would be no real damage to our earth.

Today, there is a virtual consensus among the global scientific community that the earth's atmosphere does not have a limitless amount of space to absorb pollution. The sky is the limit but we also know that the sky is not limitless. The earth's atmosphere contains a finite amount of space. Rapid industrialization and increasing amounts of greenhouse gas emissions are likely to result in global warming, with possibly disastrous consequences for many parts of the world. If sea levels rise, as they are expected to, island states like the Maldives, whose highest point is five feet above sea level, could disappear.

The 6.3 billion occupants of the planet earth are therefore increasingly aware that they are caught in a global village that has in turn been encased in a glass greenhouse with a limited amount of atmosphere. The rich houses in the village pollute more. The poor houses pollute less, but as their income levels rise, their levels of pollution are expected to rise. China and India have 2.5 billion people. Both are likely to succeed economically. Hence their per-capita pollution levels will inevitably rise. If their per-capita pollution levels rise to even half American levels, it would almost certainly be a disaster for the finite atmosphere in the greenhouse in which the global village is trapped. Already there are indications that Asian pollution has traveled to North America. According to an article in the *International Herald Tribune*:

> Scientists engaged in a major study of air quality and climate change have discovered pollutants from Asia hanging high over New England and the Atlantic this summer—one of the early surprises of research aimed at clarifying how smokestack and auto emissions travel and change in the atmosphere.
>
> The discovery is the first observation of Asian pollution plumes over the East Coast of North America and it suggests that improvements in American air quality could be threatened as Asian countries rapidly become more industrialized, one lead researcher said.
>
> "We have to be concerned whether the cost of continuing to ratchet up emission controls is not going to be offset by growing pollution coming to us from Asia," said Daniel Jacob, a Harvard university researcher who is serving as deputy mission scientist

for the intensive, six-week study. "At some point it may be cheaper to sell pollution control to China."

Given this dire prospect, it would have been natural for the richest members of the global village to encourage the poorest members to develop their economies responsibly by paying attention to the levels of per-capita pollution they will generate. The only way to convince them to be more responsible is by leading through example. The rich members would do well to commit themselves to reducing per-capita emission levels to encourage the poorer members to commit themselves to increasing their per-capita emissions slowly and carefully. This would have been a sensible global compromise.

Such a compromise was attempted when the nations of the world negotiated and agreed to the Kyoto Protocol in October 1997. The Kyoto Protocol could have formed the basis for more agreements on how to manage the limited amount of atmosphere in the greenhouse. But it has virtually died since the United States announced its decision not to ratify the agreement. The Bush administration, which came into office in 2001, after the Kyoto agreement had been signed, declared that the agreement was lopsided in not imposing any obligation on the poor developing countries. Hence it walked away from it.

Some of the American criticisms of the Kyoto agreement are valid. It can be improved, but not if America plays no part in the agreement. As China and India develop, it is only fair for them to share some of the burdens of controlling pollution. But as the lead polluter, America has to lead by example and show its willingness to sacrifice some of its polluting activities. But by walking away from the Kyoto agreement without suggesting any viable alternative or another compromise, America has doomed the world to moving towards unchecked pollution. The global village is going to be trapped in an increasingly polluted glass greenhouse, not a happy prospect.

While the Kyoto agreement's failure to include any obligation on the developing countries provided a reasonable excuse for the United States to walk away from the agreement, the real reason why the United States walked away from the Kyoto agreement is that no American leader could persuade the American political system, which is tied to specific and short-term vested interests, to agree to making the kind of sacrifices that would be needed for America to lead by example in reducing per-capita emissions. No politician in America gets elected by suggesting that the American voters should make domestic sacrifices to help create a new global consensus. Instead, more politicians are elected in America by thumbing their nose at the world and declaring that they would not lead America into accepting any restrictions imposed by global needs. Here again, democracy is destiny.

An Albert Einstein might propose a fifty-cent solution to this global environmental problem. A fifty-cent-per-gallon tax on gasoline consumption would lead to enormous benefits: reduce gas consumption, encourage increased fuel efficiency, reduce pollution, raise significant revenues that could in turn be put into an Environment Trust Fund to help American industries adjust their manufacturing processes to reduce emission levels and help protect workers against job losses. Equally importantly, reduced American dependence on Middle East oil would change the geopolitical chemistry of the world and lead to less involvement of America in the oil-rich Islamic Arab societies.

The benefits both for America and for the rest of the world of a fifty-cent-per-gallon tax would be enormous. Under any political or economic calculus, the benefits would far outweigh the costs. But there would be one significant cost. To get the proposal moving, an

American politician would have to commit political suicide by making the proposal and pushing for its adoption. Since no American politician wants to commit political suicide, the fifty-cent-per-gallon solution will never get off the ground. Consequently, as global pollution levels rise, led by America and with the rest of the world racing to catch up, there will be increased tensions as America and the rest of the world blame each other on environmental issues. Unless America leads by example, the global community will be caught in a vicious downward spiral.

A shrinkage of physical space is easy to visualize and be conscious of. Many of us have been stuck in crowds in small spaces. The idea of a shrinking physical environment is intuitively not difficult to absorb. What is difficult to absorb is the notion of a shrinking "political space." But this too is an inevitable consequence of globalization. Events and issues can have immediate political impact in opposite corners of the world. One reason why political turbulence will grow in the twenty-first century is that many "domestic" political actions will have global ramifications.

The Middle East issue is the clearest example. A few decades ago, the political repercussions of a dispute between the Israelis and the Palestinians would have been confined to the neighboring countries. Since 1967, as the Arab leaders found the Israeli-Palestinian dispute a convenient political issue to use to improve their domestic political standing, the dispute began to resonate in the larger Arab world also.

Since the 1970s, and conspicuously since 1980, for a complex basket of reasons, the Israeli-Palestinian issue has become "wired" to a political grid that weaves its way into communities all over the world. It is no exaggeration to say that any major development in the Middle East issue has electrifying effects in many parts of the world. Indeed, to use a common American metaphor, the Israeli-

Palestinian issue has become "the third rail" of both American politics and Islamic societies all around the world. But it has become "the third rail" in exactly opposite ways.

Within America, when a political decision has to be made on any facet of the Israeli-Palestinian issue, the political or intellectual merits of the issue are virtually irrelevant. The domestic implications override other considerations. Hence, when Prime Minister Ariel Sharon visited America in April 2004, the close political contest developing between George W. Bush and John Kerry dictated President Bush's response. He endorsed Sharon's plan for a total pullout from Gaza as well as Sharon's plans to retain some settlements in the West Bank, even though this was against the U.N. Security Council Resolutions 242 and 338 which had hitherto formed the basis for American policy on an Israeli-Palestinian settlement. This American move upset many European governments. Javier Solana, the chief European Union spokesman on foreign policy issues, responded to the change in U.S. policy by reiterating Europe's stance that Israel should return to its pre-1967 boundaries unless Palestine agrees to change them: "Final status issues can only be resolved by mutual agreement between the parties." However, no American politician spoke up to criticize the shift in American policy. The Kerry camp brainstormed this issue and, as a very senior Democrat foreign policy adviser said at an informal meeting afterwards, the "E" word was taboo: the Democrats could not support an "*Even-handed*" policy on the Middle East issue because, in key states like Florida, neither Bush nor Kerry could afford to alienate American Jewish voters in any way. In short, domestic political considerations dictated an American response to a foreign policy issue that had become hot-wired globally.

At the same time, in a country of about the same size and population as America, another close election was being fought out: in Indonesia. Traditionally, Indonesians had paid little attention to the

Israeli-Palestinian issue. But as a result of the shrinking globe and increasing global information flows, the Israeli-Palestinian issue had also become "the third rail" of Indonesian politics. No Indonesian leader could afford to be seen to be soft in his or her support for the Palestinians. This would have been as politically suicidal for any aspiring Indonesian politician as it would have been for any American politician to be seen as soft in his support for Israel. Remarkably, less than a decade earlier, the then Indonesian President Suharto was able to receive Prime Minister Yitzhak Rabin of Israel in Jakarta after the successful talks brokered by Bill Clinton between Arafat and Rabin. A mere decade later, such a visit had become inconceivable. Domestic political considerations in Indonesia killed any possibility of rapprochement with Israel.

American scholars often lament the fact that very few societies in the Third World, especially in the Islamic world, have established strong democratic political systems. This is true. But in making such an observation, American scholars ignore a truly important seismic shift that has taken place in Islamic societies. There has been little democratization of political structures. But there has been a profound democratization of the political spirit of these societies. As recently as a few decades ago, few Islamic or Arab rulers (most of whom were strictly authoritarian) would pay attention to the sentiments of the street. Today, even the most authoritarian rulers have to pay attention to the sentiments of the Islamic or Arab streets, as most of their citizens watch television and are educated daily on the inequities suffered by Muslims in Palestine or Bosnia, Chechnya or Iraq. This has narrowed the political options for Islamic leaders on any international issue that has become "hotwired" into their domestic political grid.

The tragedy here is that the outlines of a solution to the Israeli-Palestinian problem have never been clearer. These outlines were well-captured in the plans that Crown Prince Abdullah pulled out from his drawer to hand over to Tom Friedman, the *New York Times* columnist, which Friedman then published in his column on February 17, 2002. Both Israel and Palestine would recognize each other as states and reconfigure the borders spelled out in U.N. Security Council Resolutions 242 and 338. Friedman was understandably elated to receive this plan from Crown Prince Abdullah. As he said in his column then, "Crown Prince Abdullah seemed to be signaling that if President Bush took a new initiative for Middle East peace, he and other Arab leaders would be prepared to do so as well."

A solution to the Arab-Israeli issue would have undercut one of the central arguments of this book: that the world could unwittingly create new political structures and systems that will deliver decades of turbulence in the twenty-first century. The plans exist—but they have never been acted upon. In the two-plus years that have passed since Crown Prince Abdullah handed over his peace plan to Friedman, the further "democratization" of the political processes in North America and the Islamic world have made it even more difficult for politicians to approach the difficult, concessionary middle ground.

This is a fundamental global contradiction that we have created: by deepening the structures or the spirit of democratization in most domestic societies, each society has become politically motivated to make decisions that serve the short-term and immediate interest of voters. Yet at the same time, we are creating daily thicker and thicker webs of interdependence, where the needs and interests of one nation, or electorate, overlap another. We live in a global village but we elect only leaders who take care of our own home. We are therefore creating simultaneously a growing need for global governance while at the same time strengthening structures and processes that prevent it. This is a prescription for instability.

All this does not mean that American power will not prevail in global decisionmaking processes. There is always a time lag in history. Hence the propensity of multilateral institutions that were designed to enhance American power at the time of American dominance will continue to operate. Most of the decisions that these institutions will make most of the time will reflect American power. The world will not change dramatically because of the global contradiction that I have described above. But over time, there will be a major shift in how American power is perceived.

Most American strategic thinkers, given the nature of the education and training that they receive, believe that American power primarily rests on military foundations. Other forms of American power can be resisted. The political and economic power of America has not proved adequate to unseat either Castro or Kim Jong Il. But American military power is irresistible, as Saddam Hussein discovered (and as Gadaffi of Libya began to understand after the invasion of Iraq). And the gap between American military power and that of the rest of the world is growing rather than diminishing. The American military budget will soon be larger than that of the rest of the world combined. America's technological lead over the rest of the world in the military field is also growing. No army or navy or air force can confront its American equivalent head on and survive.

An unexpected consequence taking place in America is that this trend towards greater military supremacy is coupled simultaneously with a sense of greater personal insecurity. In part this was a result of 9/11, the first direct assault on the American mainland from across the ocean in centuries. This is also a result of all the intense security checks that Americans have to undergo when they board a plane or enter any nationally important building or monument. The Statue of Liberty, the very symbol of the American spirit of freedom and independence, was until recently out of bounds to American citizens.

Some of this shrinkage of "personal space of freedom" can be explained by growing fears of terrorism. Some of it can also be attributed to a shrinking sense of psychological space that comes from an awareness of sharing a shrinking planet with billions of other citizens who are also clamoring for increased space of their own. But if the argument of this book is correct, some of the "shrinkage of personal space" comes from an awareness (which is now growing more in the subconscious than the conscious realms) that the "legitimacy" of American power is also diminishing. Americans are beginning to feel that they are less "liked."

The official American intelligence community is aware of the rising levels of anti-Americanism. In 2002 and 2003, I attended two conferences on this subject organized by the National Intelligence Council at the lovely Wye River Plantation Conference site. In both conferences, I may have come across as one of the most optimistic foreign participants. At both conferences, I emphasized that on balance, the levels of pro-Americanism all around the world were still higher than the levels of anti-Americanism. But I also added that the trend was negative, and that something had to be done to arrest it.

Those two conferences and several others made me realize that there is a strong desire on the part of American intellectuals to believe that this problem of rising levels of anti-Americanism is a "passing shower." They argue that America has gone through such bad patches before, as it did during the Vietnam War. Hence, this will also pass. Many also believe that the rising levels of anti-Americanism are the result of what they perceive to be the insensitive international policies of the Bush administration in particular. They hope and believe that if the neocons are removed from office and replaced by a gentler and kinder administration, the problem of rising levels of anti-Americanism would gradually disappear. It is difficult to convince these people that they are dealing not with a passing problem but a possible tectonic shift.

One way to describe the danger that America faces is to describe it as the danger of the "Sovietization" of American power. What truly distinguished American power from Soviet power both during and after the Cold War was that American power was always perceived to be more "legitimate" in the eyes of most of the international community. Most Americans would like to believe that this was a natural result of the supremacy of American ideology over Soviet Marxist ideology.

In theory, however, Soviet Marxist ideology should have been more appealing than American capitalist ideology to the masses of the world. The Soviet model was based upon the ideal of liberating the masses from exploitation; the American model was built on the idea of each individual seeking his own profit and gain. The Soviet Marxists espoused an idea of a community working together to serve the collective interests; the American capitalists espoused an ideal of the individual's right to seek the greatest degree of freedom and independence. In its extreme form, as espoused by Ayn Rand, the phrase was "greed is good." These are caricatures of what were clearly complex ideological mixes. But in theory, at least, the Soviet ideological model was not inherently inferior to the American ideological model.

In practice, however, there was no doubt that the American model was far superior to the Soviet model, not only because it delivered a higher standard of living and greater affluence. More importantly, the eyes of the world could see that the Soviet people were held together by the brute force of a totalitarian state. No happy Marxist community existed there. Ironically, if Marx were reborn during the Cold War, he would have found the American community of free and independent spirits coming together to cooperate out of individual volition rather than by diktats of the state closer to his ideal vision of a Marxist community of free spirits. The affluence and general happiness of the American people were the best advertisements for capitalism.

In its dealings with the rest of the world, the Soviet Union showed a brutal and hard face. Most of its allies on its periphery stayed within the Soviet sphere not out of free will but under duress. Given a choice, most would have walked away from the Soviet bloc. By contrast, most of America's allies were allies by choice. They were happy to participate in the international order created by America that provided for prosperity for American people and for their own citizens. For most countries, an alliance with America was a win-win partnership; an alliance with the Soviet Union was a win-lose partnership, with only the Soviet Union winning.

When the Cold War ended, most Americans (and probably most non-Americans then too) felt that nothing fundamental had changed. The circle of free and independent countries had merely expanded. The former allies of the Soviet Union, especially in East Europe, rushed to join American-led or American-inspired communities like NATO or the European Union. They embraced the American ideal of win-win partnerships.

But a major shift in American policies took place at the end of the Cold War. Most of the incentives that America had for creating win-win partnerships disappeared. Hence, while the form of many Cold War relationships remained the same, the substance of these relationships began to change. Gradually, more and more countries (like Pakistan and Thailand) found that their long history of cooperation with America during the Cold War no longer mattered to America. Those partnerships that were valuable when America needed to confront the Soviet Union became liabilities rather than assets, carrying political and economic costs with few apparent dividends, once the Cold War was won.

There was nothing devious or perfidious about this U-turn in American posture towards the rest of the world. Viewed under the cold light of reason, one could agree that this American move was both rational and justifiable in terms of American national self-interest. The prevailing rules of the international order go back to the Treaty of Westphalia, which recognized that each nation should be allowed to advance its national interests. Altruism was not built into the deal. Win-win partnerships were allowed. But so too were zero-sum games when the more powerful state, if it had the power to do so, could try to bend the international order to serve its interests. As the Cold War ended, American policymakers began to realize that America had far greater power than any other country in the world. And the temptation to bend the international order to serve American national interests became greater with each passing year. The international system had not developed any checks and balances to counter this huge American power. No one knew how to. And the power began to be asserted more often.

While there were no formal checks and balances to unilateral use of American power, there was one force emerging to counter it. Ironically, this force had also been unleashed globally by America: the force of American ideals. Any intelligent soul living anywhere in the world in the post–Cold War era believed that the best way of life in the planet was the American way of life. These intelligent souls flocked to American universities to study. Indeed, as a result of American generosity in opening up its universities to the elites of the world, America has successfully educated and opened the eyes of these elites. They understood both the philosophical underpinnings and the language of American social science, whether it be in the political, economic, social, or legal fields. They learned one of the most important insights of American social science: Always describe political and economic realities as they are, not how you wish them to be.

The rising level of knowledge and understanding all around the world is in many ways the result of America's export of its ideas and ideals to the rest of the world. It is hard to imagine how the current dramatic transformation under way in both China and India could have occurred without their elites having been transformed by their immersion in or contact with the American way of life. America has successfully Americanized the elites of the world. But having been Americanized, they hold the American government to the same high standards abroad that Americans hold their own government to at home. This has created an obvious and acute tension. The American government was structurally designed to serve the interests of the American people, not the interests of the Americanized non-American elites of the world. This has inevitably led to massive disillusionment with America. The most disappointed are the most Americanized, a curious consequence of frustrated enthusiasm. America has given them intelligent eyes and minds. They are now using them to expect the best American standards of America.

If the Americanization of the elites of the world continues to grow as a result of America generously sharing its universities with the rest of the world, and if America continues to use its power to only protect or enhance its short-term national interests in a shrinking global community, the logical result will be growing waves of disillusionment. Over time, these waves of disillusionment will lead to the delegitimization of American power in the eyes of the rest of the world.

This will not happen immediately. The reservoir of legitimacy that American power rests on today will last some time yet. But 9/11 also demonstrated that something fundamental has changed in the way America is perceived by the rest of the world. I was in Manhattan on the day it happened. I felt directly the shock, anger, and anguish of Americans on that day. I could also feel their enormous sense of bewilderment and incomprehension that someone would want to kill thousands of innocent American and foreign citizens. What had they done to harm the world? Hadn't America done so much instead to benefit it?

In the three years that have passed since 9/11, I have had the opportunity to discuss that day's events with people from all over the world. Publicly most countries' governments and peoples have expressed sympathy and support for the victims of 9/11. In private, however, I have discovered a much greater variety of reactions. What has truly struck me is the high degree of quiet satisfaction I have heard over the fact that America too had finally felt some of the pain and hurt that so many people around the world take as part of their existential condition.

The gradual "delegitimization" of American power means that when Americans travel overseas or gradually begin to understand how they are viewed, they will have to deal with the contrast between their own image of themselves as benevolent global citizens and the realization that the rest of the world views them as citizens of a potentially aggressive power. Over time, there will be political and economic and even military and security costs of this growing delegitimization of American power. But in the short run, the first painful reality that Americans will have to deal with is a gradual loss of national self-esteem in a shrinking global village.

The use of the word "legitimacy" is inherently difficult in the international context. Indeed, Professor Thomas M. Franck, one of the world's most distinguished scholars on international law, has written an entire book on the subject, entitled *The Power of Legitimacy Among Nations.* In his opening chapter, he described how elusive the concept of legitimacy is when it is applied in the international arena.

In the domestic context, the actions of individuals and organizations are deemed to be legitimate when certain procedures are complied with. Hence, the rule of any American president or the law-enacting capacity of the U.S. Congress is deemed to be "legitimate" if the officials had been constitutionally elected by the people. Similarly, the decisions of the U.S. Supreme Court are deemed to be "legitimate" if the justices are confirmed by the Senate and their decisions do not violate the principles of the constitution. Domestically, it is often easy to figure out which actions are legitimate and which are not. Adherence to the right "procedures" determines the legitimacy of any decision.

This focus on the procedural aspects of legitimacy ignores one important dimension: in the final analysis, it is the judgment of the people that matters. Occasionally, even when all the correct procedures are followed, the decision reached can be "legal," but not necessarily "legitimate." For example, O. J. Simpson went through an exhaustive trial when he was charged with the murder of his wife. The court pronounced him not guilty. This decision was "legal," but in the eyes of many, it was not perceived to be "legitimate." Legitimacy, to make a controversial point, lies in the eyes of the beholder. Today, as the 6.3 billion citizens of the planet are increasingly beginning to be aware that they belong to a single global village (to use Kofi Annan's phrase once again), they are also moving towards making judgments on the "legitimacy" or "illegitimacy" of global decisions and events. It is these 6.3 billion pairs of eyes that are the ultimate custodians of legitimacy in the international environment. There may not be adequate international processes and procedures to ascertain legitimacy. But as a rising tide of common sense envelops the world, it is also clear that it is possible to discern today what events and processes enjoy legitimacy.

The recent Iraq war provides a good example of how international attitudes towards legitimacy are evolving. The Iraq war was controversial within America. In the traditional American fashion, there was a debate about the war. But when the U.S. Congress passed legislation authorizing the war, there were no further questions on the legitimacy of the war. No major American figure went to the U.S. Supreme Court to ascertain whether the war was legal. All this showed that despite the disagreements, the American polity reached the conclusion that the decision to go to war was legitimate.

The global polis (to use a phrase used in Professor Thomas Franck's book) reached the opposite conclusion. In their eyes, the war was deemed to be illegitimate on several counts. Firstly, both the United States and the United Kingdom made a decision (and this may have been a flawed decision) to go to the U.N. Security Council to seek a resolution authorizing the use of force against Iraq. They failed to get a resolution. Despite this, they went to war. This was a shock to the global polis, as both countries were perceived to be violating the principle governing the use of force that America had put into place at the end of World War II. As Fareed Zakaria noted (in a review of the book by Hans Blix, the famous U.N. arms inspector), the United States did not seem to care about international legitimacy. He wrote, "Every country—yes, even France—was coming around to the view that the inspections needed to go on for only another month or two, that benchmarks could have been established, and if the Iraqis failed these tests the Security Council would authorize war. But in a fashion that is almost reminiscent of World War I, the Pentagon's military timetables drove American diplomacy. The weather had become more important than international legitimacy."[6] Secondly, the key justification for the war was the claim that Saddam Hussein was hiding weapons of mass destruction (WMD) in violation of U.N. Security Council resolutions. After the invasion, no WMD were found. This shocked the international community. Thirdly, after the invasion, the occupying force botched the occupation. The decision to protect the oil ministry and not the fabled antiquities of Iraq in the Baghdad Museum sent a powerful negative signal.

The key point to emphasize here is that intelligent minds were watching those events around the globe and passing judgment on the war in Iraq. On the one hand, they knew that America was not an imperial power. It had no desire to invade or occupy other countries. The American people only wanted to help the Iraqi people, not harm them. On the other hand, they saw the clear violation of established principles of international law and the failure to find any WMD to justify the war. Any American walking down the street in any corner of the globe would have been hard put to find a supporter of the war. There may have been a majority consensus among the general publics in virtually every other country in the world (including in countries that supported the war, like the UK, Spain, and Poland) that the invasion of Iraq was *not* legitimate.

But when the American government sent clear signals that it had learned from its original mistakes and realized that it had to work with and not against the international community in finding a solution in Iraq, the perceptions of the American action began to change. The U.N.'s involvement was key. The unanimous Security Council resolution in support of a new approach, the direct involvement of Kofi Annan and his special envoy, Lakhdar Brahimi, and the close consultations with the Iraqi people showed that America was not acting unilaterally or arbitrarily. At the same time, the international community was also aware that any failure in Iraq would not just damage Iraq. It would provide a psychological boost to the radical Islamic terrorist groups who would profit from a perception that America had been "humiliated" in Iraq. Hence, the perception of the American presence in Iraq began to shift. The initial invasion was not perceived to be legitimate. The subsequent efforts to find a viable solution in Iraq that would be acceptable to both the Iraqi people and the international community were perceived to be legitimate.

In short, the international community is capable of making sophisticated and nuanced judgments on the legitimacy of actions. Tom Friedman has described how Israel regained its legitimacy in its struggle against Hezbollah when it withdrew from Lebanon. He quotes Shibley Telhami, Middle East studies professor at the University of Maryland: "In every conflict, the extent to which a party can muster domestic support and international support, and the extent to which its public will withstand higher thresholds of pain, is very much a function of the degree of international legitimacy for that cause. As soon as Israel withdrew from Lebanon to the internationally recognized border, the legitimacy factor shifted from Hezbollah to Israel. This may seem abstract, but it's not." Friedman hence concluded, "When you have legitimacy on your side, your people, and the world, support you more, and the other side's people, and the world, support them less."[7]

The remarkable thing about the Iraq war was the relative sophistication of international commentaries compared to the relative lack of sophistication of American commentaries on the war. Certainly, post–9/11, the boundaries of debate within America on national security issues have narrowed. This narrowing is unfortunate. In the shrinking global village, America is now sharing political space with a sophisticated international community (many of whom were trained in American universities). The time has come for America to match the sophistication of the international community in passing judgment on the common global challenges that mankind faces. The insularity of the American debate has to end.

A few sophisticated American political commentators have begun to acknowledge that they were perhaps somewhat naive in their judgment of the Iraq issue before America went to war there. David Brooks, a self-described conservative columnist in the *New York Times*, wrote this on April 17, 2004:

> . . . Most of all, I misunderstood how normal Iraqis would react to our occupation. I knew they'd resent us. But I thought they would see that our interests and their interests are aligned. We both want to establish democracy and get the U.S. out.
>
> I did not appreciate how our very presence in Iraq would overshadow democratization. Now I get the sense that while the Iraqis don't want us to fail, since our failure would mean their failure, many don't want to see us succeed either. They want to

see us bleed, to get taken down a notch, to suffer for their chaos and suffering. A democratic Iraq is an abstraction they want for the future; the humiliation of America is a pleasure they can savor today.

In these few lines, Brooks described well the chasm that separates well-intentioned Americans from the people that they are trying to help. So how many people are there in the world who want to "savor" the humiliation of America? Their numbers are rising, for sure. If America wishes to reverse this trend, it must understand why American good intentions can prove so damaging, especially if they are linked to a general ignorance and indifference to the interests and concerns of the rest of mankind.

The danger here is that if the delegitimization of American power in the eyes of the world continues to grow, there will be real costs for America and its people. Increased terrorism is only one of the more obvious. The full economic costs have not yet been fully weighed and understood.

It would, however, be a mistake to focus only on economic or material costs of such delegitimization. Most of us get our sense of well-being from our integration into and acceptance by the community we belong to. In some ways, Americans understand the value of communities better than any other people because virtually all the communities they belong to are results of free choice. This is why American communities, in virtually all areas, social, civic, academic, are more vibrant than their counterparts anywhere else in the world. We cherish more the community we choose to belong to than the community thrust upon us. The best of communities are held together not by coercion but by a common sense of identity based on shared values.

This therefore is the ultimate challenge for America in the twenty-first century: to take all the experience it has learnt from creating vibrant voluntary communities based on shared values on American soil and apply this experience globally. The world already admires deeply many of the values that American society is built upon. Most Americans know intuitively how to create a vibrant community on their soil. Why can't the same principles and values be applied in trying to create a global community?

The values that underpin the American sense of community include a belief in certain inalienable rights of each human being and a conviction that a good society can only be built when each citizen is free and independent and where each citizen also believes that she or he has an equal opportunity. These were the values that enabled America to fight a civil war and triumph in the struggle to end slavery. It was these values that led to the civil rights movement that finally delivered equal political opportunities to blacks and whites. And it was these values that restrained America from becoming a colonial power.

The real challenge therefore for America is to extend membership in this community of values to all the citizens of the globe. Only by appreciating and supporting the diversity and individuality of other cultures—Muslim, Hindu, Chinese, South American—can America credibly be the architect of such a community. America did not intend to change the world. But it did. It shrank the world. In so doing, it has created a global community. Traditionally our moral concerns have stopped at our borders. When a hurricane hits Louisiana, Americans feel an obligation to respond and help. But when it hits Haiti across the sea, they feel a lesser obligation to respond. When it strikes in the South Pacific, they do not know about it at all.

In the borderless world unleashed by America, the notion that narrow, short-term national self-interest should wall in moral concerns seems anachronistic. None of us would want to live in a community where each household takes care only of its own interests and concerns and ignores (or even jeopardizes) the interests and concerns of the community. But this is how the prevailing rules of the international order work: each nation for itself; no nation for the global community. Having changed the world, America has both an obligation and an enlightened long-term self-interest in forging a real sense of community among all the nations and peoples of the world to ensure that they too defend not just their immediate national interests but the common global interests.

This move is nothing more than another logical step up the human evolutionary ladder. We began with taking care only of our own families and clans. Then we organized ourselves into villages. From villages, we moved on to larger social units, forging either city-states or nation-states. At each step, it seemed inconceivable that we could ever give up a part of our local identities in favor of a larger grouping. The Welsh, the Scots, and the Irish still want to preserve their identities. But they also acknowledge the benefits that flow from being citizens of a common polity, the United Kingdom and the European Union. The ultimate destination in this natural process of human existence is the development of a sense of community among mankind. We are not there yet but given the many problems we face in common, we have no choice but to create a real sense of community among the more than six billion inhabitants of the earth. This is the ultimate challenge that our world faces. It is inconceivable that America could ignore this challenge. It is even less conceivable that America would be unaffected if this challenge is not met.

~ 7 ~

The Way Ahead

*I*NTUITIVELY, as most of us look down the twenty-first century, we can feel a certain unease about the future we are walking into. In the 1990s, when we seemed to be living in a blessed decade, we tended to assume that the future could only look bright. 9/11 shattered that assumption. Today, as we try to look at the state of the planet as a whole, we see a troubled world. Our sense of a well-ordered universe has gone. It has been replaced by an awareness that things may be spinning out of control, that many problems have effectively become borderless, from terrorism to the SARS virus. In a globalized economy, jobs slide from one country to another, even from one continent to another. Financial flows are increasing both in volume and in speed. Each day, we wake to a greater sense of uncertainty about the future. We are inclined to believe that we are slipping and sliding towards a more dangerous world.

The simple truth is that it is not beyond the capacity of America, working together with the rest of the world, to create a more stable world order. America has more than enough resources to bring this about. But America will not carry the burden of the world on its shoulders alone. As a result of the remarkable transformation of the world that beneficent American policies have brought about over the past century or so, there is now a thick band of middle-class citizens around the world who share the interests of the American people in bringing about a stable world order. These are the children of the American century. The dream that they have for themselves and for their children is the American dream: to have a comfortable home with all the modern amenities and opportunities, both in education and employment. They want their children to do better than they have and they share the American desire to live according to ideals and beliefs they choose for themselves. This is true even in the Islamic world. Given a choice, those in the middle class and those approaching the middle class would like the world around them to become more stable so that they can pursue these dreams. They would like to walk into shopping malls and onto aircraft with no fear of bombs going off. The world is full of reasonable people who want to help create a stable order. The main question they have in their minds is whether America will provide the leadership to bring this about.

This is a real question. On the one hand, the country that has done more both to bring about globalization and to educate the world about its consequences is America. The conceptual tools and the information resources of American social scientists have explained how much the world has changed. President Bill Clinton has been very forceful in arguing that the world has moved "from interdependence to integration." In speeches that I have given in various corners of America, I often use the image of the boat that I mentioned in the introduction to this volume. Few Americans resist the notion that we are all now passengers on the same boat. They feel the impact of the rest of the world on their daily lives. Yet they also feel uncomfortable when I suggest that if we are all passengers on the same boat, we need a captain or crew to man this common boat. The idea that we need to have better management of global issues has not yet sunk into American consciousness. Thus, Americans both want a more stable world order and do not want to think about how to bring it about. This leads to questions around the world whether there is sufficient wisdom within the American body politic to provide leadership for global stability.

Many would like to believe that this job is both too difficult and too enormous for America to do alone. In fact, the job can be done. It will take some effort, perhaps even a little sacrifice, but it will not be too much. There are a few critical strategic decisions that America has to make.

The first strategic decision may seem obvious and common-sensical: America first has to *decide* that a stable world order is in America's interests. In their rhetoric, American leaders never hesitate to mention that they support global stability. But in its deeds vis-à-vis the rest of the world, America sends mixed messages. This is why it is possible to have entire books written about America's impact on the world order and end up with almost exactly opposite conclusions. Professor Anne-Marie Slaughter has published a persuasive new book called *A New World Order,* which describes how many American policies have had a stabilizing impact on the world. As she said, "The United States has taken the lead in insisting that many international problems have domestic roots and that they be addressed at that level—within nations rather than simply between them—but it is also coming to understand the vital need to address those problems multilaterally rather than unilaterally, for reasons of legitimacy, burden sharing and effectiveness."[1] Hence, many American practices promote world order. On the other hand, Clyde

Prestowitz produced at about the same time a book entitled *Rogue Nation*, which catalogued the destructive effects of many American practices on the world.

Both books are accurate in describing American policies and practices, since one can find both stabilizing and destabilizing elements, often in the same actions. The essential problem is that there is no built-in coherence in American policies towards the world because no major strategic decision has yet been taken to achieve such coherence. Each decision is made on the basis of specific short-term considerations, pushed by specific constituents like the textile manufacturers in North Carolina or the automobile manufacturers who insist that the SUVs, designed to carry passengers, be given the same tax treatment as trucks.

The time to make such a strategic decision is now. The world has not turned irreversibly against America. One of the biggest contributions that America has made to the world has been to increase the intelligence and sophistication of the elites and populations passing judgment on America. They can see whether American policies are formulated with their interests or concerns in mind. They can distinguish form from substance, rhetoric from reality. This increasing intelligence and sophistication is an asset that America can use to its advantage.

Not long ago the world was full of admiration and respect for America: Clearly America had done some things right. America needs to develop a comprehensive and sophisticated understanding of the many ways in which it has benefited the world. Professor Joseph Nye has written brilliantly and convincingly about the "soft power" American projects around the world. But "soft power" alone cannot win hearts and minds. There must be an alignment between the impact of American "hard power" and "soft power." If they work at cross-purposes, as has happened in recent years, the rest of the world will grow skeptical of America's "soft power," viewing it as an increasingly frayed velvet glove that covers a mailed fist. The rest of the world will not reach out to a mailed fist. The point here is a simple one: Deeds matter as much as, if not more than, words.

The second strategic decision that America has to make flows from the first. Whenever the American government makes any major decision, it should take into consideration the international impact of its decisions. To put it simply, it should apply the Law of *Intended* International Consequences. The word "intended" may cause some confusion. Most of the time, when America makes its decisions it does not "intend" (in the sense of being consciously aware of such an intention) to harm anybody else. When it gives subsidies to its cotton farmers, it does not "intend" to harm West African farmers. When it keeps gas prices low to ensure that its politicians get reelected, it does not "intend" to harm the world by causing global warming. Surely these adverse international consequences should be more accurately described as "unintended" rather than "intended."

In a world where we are ignorant of the impact of our actions, it may be possible to argue that these adverse consequences were unintended. But America has done more than any other country to abolish this universe of ignorance. It has planted intelligent minds (trained in the best American universities) in every corner of the globe. These discerning minds, as a result of their training and experience, follow American affairs very closely. They can observe the American decision-making processes and see whether their interests and concerns are taken into consideration or not. They can also read the *New York Times* editorials on cotton subsidies or global warming. Hence they are puzzled by claims made by American policymakers that they did not "intend" to harm anyone else with their policies. How could they be less well-informed than graduates of American universities who live overseas?

Julian Hewitt, president of AIESEC, South Africa, a student-run organization focused on developing global change-agents, wrote a commentary, first published in the *Boston Globe*, in which he expressed astonishment at the ignorance of Americans over the impact they have on the world. He said:

> The ultimate global power, the United States creates ripples that cause big waves around the world. This happens more frequently than the average American comprehends. When the Federal Reserve chairman, Alan Greenspan, cuts interest rates by a quarter of a percentage point, it has a huge impact on me in South Africa. Straightaway, it influences my still sizable student loan, as the South African financial markets react to this news by pre-empting a cut or a hike by the South African Reserve Bank. In short, globalization enables Greenspan's small action to have a large effect on me 13,000 miles away in South Africa. Imagine how many other powerful decisions resonate with me as a citizen of South Africa. When the United States refuses to sign the Kyoto Protocol, it forces me to apply a few more layers of sunscreen in the summer. When the United States attacks Iraq, it heightens the religious animosity between the large Muslim and Christian communities living near Cape Town. Hollywood movies, music, multinationals, foreign policy, farming subsidies, and import tariffs have a similar effect. These endless ripples are reaching my distant shore. As I spend time in the United States, however, I am discovering some startling realities . . . .

> The average American gets little information about what is happening in the world or about the role of the United States in world events. Twenty or thirty years ago, there would be nothing wrong with an American who never left home, never owned a passport, never spoke a second language, never knew the capital

of Denmark. But we live in a globalized world. We live in a world of causes and effects. We live in a world where a single super-power has an overwhelming influence on global affairs. It is dangerous to be the source of global ripples but to ignore their effects. Over time, those ripples may cause waves that will slap back on your shores.[2]

Since ignorance is no longer an excuse in a universe where information is abundant, America should develop the habit of applying the Law of *Intended* International Consequences when it formulates and implements major policies. This is a habit that any household employs when it lives in a crowded village. No household throws its garbage across the fence if it knows that just beyond the fence is a neighbor. America has shrunk the world and created a small crowded global village. Virtually every other nation is trying to adjust to living in such a small global village. The world expects America to do the same. Indeed, if the American population was made aware that it was harming other countries, it would be among the first to protest against these policies. Hence the challenge for American policymakers is to take advantage of the reservoir of good intentions that the American people have towards the world and translate those good intentions into concrete policies.

It is essential to emphasize that while the really poor countries expect America to be more generous in its aid flows (and in per capita terms America's Overseas Development Assistance (ODA) contributions are among the lowest in the industrialized world), most of the world is not asking for handouts. Most of the time, all they are asking for is a level playing field. They believe in the American tradition of fair play. Hence, they would like America to shape an international order where all countries, big and small, rich and poor, have a relatively level playing field to compete on. In theory, this is what America has set out to do. In practice, as this book has tried to demonstrate, it often has not. This gap between words and deeds has to be narrowed.

But words do matter too. Deeds have consequences. So do words. Many of my American friends have told me that I should ignore the "prattle" among the chattering classes of America about the arrival of the Age of the American Empire. They dismiss it as another silly season in America that will come and go, like any other fad. But it would be unwise to underestimate the impact of this prattle, if indeed it is only prattle, about the American empire. If the word "empire" appears frequently on the cover of, say, the *New York Times Sunday Magazine*, and books on the subject of American empire make it to the best-seller lists, it does indicate that there is a strain in American thinking that does dream of the possibility of creating such an empire and perhaps enjoying some of the sweet fruits of imperialism.

Any American who dreams of empire should be aware that the very notion of creating or recreating an empire is deeply offensive to my generation of Asians who have experienced both colonial rule and the pleasures of independence. British colonial rule was by far the most benign of any European colonial rule. But even so, as one who was born a British colonial subject, I can testify that in any colonial rule (or imperial rule), there are the rulers and the ruled, the shepherd and the sheep. It is mentally debilitating to live under a condition of non-citizenship, to live in one's own land and not feel the sense of ownership over the land.

America has done more than any other country to change that grain of history unalterably. It has firmly planted the idea of equal dignity and worth of all human beings. Hence, even in countries that have struggled after the end of colonial rule, there is no desire to welcome back the old colonial rulers. In the nineteenth century, the three hundred million Indians, including my ancestors, who accepted more or less passively the British raj may have assumed that this was a natural condition. In the twenty-first century, it is inconceivable that this could happen. Few people in Asia believe today that Anglo-Saxon rule will be better for them.

America as a society is also not designed to lead an empire. To repeat, empires are built on foundations of violence. Without violent suppression from time to time, the natives get restless. No empire can be built without blood being spilled, although the aftermath can sometimes appear to be bloodless, as the British raj (in the romantic memories of many in the Anglo-Saxon world) appears to be to so many today. The British empire succeeded in surviving for a long time through a unique combination of careful use of force and deeply ingrained Machiavellian instincts, including carefully developed instincts of divide and rule.

One big lesson of the Iraq war is that America is not ready for empire. America has the military means to conquer any country. Indeed, the military invasion of Iraq was brilliant, accomplished with minimum American casualties. But the occupation has become a textbook case study of how not to occupy a country. Many mistakes were made. Perhaps the most fundamental mistake was the *assumption* that American troops would be welcomed as liberators. This assumption was deeply ingrained in many American minds because most American minds only saw Iraq through the prism of their good intentions. They forgot to ask the obvious question: Which country in the world today welcomes foreign soldiers on its soil? Two years after the invasion and occupation, Americans gradually began to understand why foreign invasion was resisted. A *New York Times* article by Edward Wong noted the following:

With just days to go before the transfer of sovereignty to the Iraqis, American commanders concede that they are far from quelling a stubborn and increasingly sophisticated insurgency. It has extended well beyond Saddam Hussein supporters and for-

eign fighters, spreading to ordinary Iraqis seething at the occupation and its failures. They act at the grassroots level, often with
little training or direction, but with a zealousness born of anti-
colonial ambitions.

The same article quoted Major-General John R. S. Batiste, com-
mander of the First Infantry division, which oversees a swath of the
northern Sunni triangle slightly larger than the state of West Vir-
ginia, as saying, "This war cannot be won militarily. It really does
need a political and economic solution."[3]

In the nineteenth century, an occupying power would have used
the horrors of Abu Ghraib to inject fear into the populace. To use
an adage, you kill the chicken to scare the monkey. But the horrors
of Abu Ghraib horrified America more than Iraq. The American
people could not stomach the idea of American troops carrying out
such acts. If America cannot tolerate the sight of its soldiers abusing
a few Iraqis, how can it build an empire? Which country will volun-
tarily welcome American or any other kind of imperial rule?

Foregoing empire does not mean that American domination of
the world will end. The sheer size of American power will ensure
American domination of the globe for decades to come. Such
power cannot be boxed in within the American borders. It will naturally flow out and affect the rest of the world. But America can significantly diminish the opposition to and the resentment of
American power by demonstrating both in words and deeds that it
will use this enormous power to serve both American and global interests. The two are not mutually exclusive. In the crowded global
village, the peace and stability of the village also serves American
interests. As Robert Wright, an American scholar, has said:

In other words, the age-old tradeoff between security and liberty
increasingly involves a third variable: antipathy. The less hatred

there is in the world, the more security we can have without sacrificing personal freedom. Assuming we like our liberty, we have little choice but to take an earnest interest in the situation of distant and seemingly strange people, working to elevate their welfare, exploring their discontent as a step toward expanding their moral horizons—and in the process expanding ours. Global governance without global moral progress could be very unpleasant. As the world's most powerful nation, and one of the world's most ethnically and religiously diverse nations, America is a natural leader of this moral revolution. America is also well positioned to lead in shaping a judicious form of global governance.[4]

The bottom line (to use a favorite term of American business) is that in our small global village, there may be a strategic alignment between American values and ideals on the one hand and long-term American national interests on the other hand. Any policy based on altruism will not last. Most human beings are prepared to make brief sacrifices or small sacrifices to act in consonance with their values. Few of us are saints. We will not sell our homes and even our hi-fi sets to feed the poor, but we may give away a small percentage of our surplus income. However, we are always prepared to either make sacrifices or put in additional efforts to safeguard our long-term interests or those of our children. This is the spirit behind the recommendations in this book, as the following parable illustrates:

Growing Good Corn

There was a farmer who grew award-winning corn. Each year he entered his corn in the state fair, where it won a blue ribbon. One year, a newspaper reporter interviewed him and learned something interesting about how he grew it. The reporter discovered that the farmer shared his seed corn with his neighbors. "How can you afford to share your best seed corn with your neighbors when they are entering corn in competition with yours each year?" the reporter asked. "Why sir," said the farmer, "didn't you know? The wind picks up pollen from the ripening corn and swirls it from field to field. If my neighbors grow inferior corn, cross-pollination will steadily degrade the quality of my corn. If I am to grow good corn, I must help my neighbors grow good corn."

He is very much aware of the connectedness of life. His corn cannot improve unless his neighbor's corn also improves. So is it in other dimensions. Those who choose to be at peace must help their neighbors to be at peace. Those who choose to live well must help others to live well, for the value of a life is measured by the lives it touches. And those who choose to be happy must help others to find happiness, for the welfare of each is bound up with the welfare of all. The lesson for each of us is this: If we are to grow good corn, we must also help our neighbours grow good corn.

What this book advocates is a policy of shared and mutual prosperity among all peoples and nations. No major sacrifices are required. A few policies (like subsidies that damage our neighbors) will have to be altered. In a small, interdependent and integrated world, consequences happen. Consequences matter. To avoid dealing with the adverse effects of consequences, we must anticipate "intended" consequences of our actions. The initial process of adjustments may appear to be painful. Some individuals may have to make short-term sacrifices (like the farmers who have profited from subsidies), but in the longer run, the overall benefits will be much higher for the world as a whole, even for the individuals who make short-term sacrifices.

The third strategic decision that America has to make therefore is to change its policies towards all multilateral institutions: It should no longer use its overwhelming power and influence within these organizations to merely serve short-term American interests. Instead, it should weigh global interests and assess the impact of its policies on the rest of the world when these multilateral institutions bend to American will.

The multilateral infrastructure that America created in 1945 was a gift to the world. It created a global framework that allowed many other nations to flourish. Today, after six decades of growth and development, these multilateral institutions could be seen as a gift to America. Over time, they have built up both legitimacy and many key operational skills. If well utilized, they could serve both America and the world well. The only key question that the world will ask is this: Are they being utilized only to serve American interests or will they also serve global interests?

Many of these institutions do need either repair or reinvention to meet the new needs of the day. In 2004, the world marked the sixtieth anniversary of the creation of two key institutions, created at the Bretton Woods resort in New Hampshire. A *Financial Times* article by Christopher Swan on May 29/30, 2004, reviewed the performance of the IMF and the World Bank. The article stated aptly that the IMF was "created as a firefighter for international crises." But when the IMF firefighters put out a financial crisis, whose interests should they factor in? Only the interests of the rich creditor countries? Or should they also take into consideration the interests of the poor countries that are in crisis? As the discussion on the Asian financial crisis showed, the IMF (at the behest of the U.S. Treasury) tried to use the occasion of the Indonesian financial crisis to reform the Indonesian political system, a reform that proved disastrous for the Indonesian people. In the same *Financial Times* article, Professor Charles Syplisg, professor of economics of the Graduate Institute of International Studies in Geneva, is quoted as saying, "There is a growing recognition that the IMF should not be interfering too deeply in sovereign affairs. When firemen come to your house to put out a blaze, you would not expect them to meddle in your marriage." This is what the IMF set out to do in Indonesia. It should avoid doing so in the future.

The selective response of the IMF to crises is also another problem. If a country is politically significant, the IMF assists. If it is not, the country is left twisting in the wind, as Thailand was. In the same *FT* article, Professor Ken Rogoff, a former chief economist of the IMF and currently an economics professor at Harvard, made another telling point about the IMF's selective responses to crises: "There has always been an exception for each country. Turkey was too Islamic to fail and Russia was too nuclear." Selectivity in helping countries in financial distress undermines the credibility of the IMF.

The IMF's primary responsibility is to maintain stability in the international financial system, which benefits America more than any other nation. This stability in turn is an essential platform to allow the expansion of world trade that has taken place over the past few decades. The IMF, despite making mistakes, has succeeded in its essential responsibilities. If it had not delivered stability to the international financial system, we would not have seen the explosion of world trade that has in turn transformed billions of lives, especially in East Asia. The performance of the IMF can be improved, as the IMF itself acknowledges today. But there is no talk of creating a whole new institution. It is true that the IMF has lost the confidence of many developing countries (who will have to also improve their own record of financial management before criticizing the IMF). But this confidence can be regained. If the IMF demonstrates that it serves global interests, not a few key national interests, it could regain the confidence of the international community. American leadership in this direction could win America some valuable goodwill.

Selective intervention also bedevils another vital international institution created by America at the end of World War II: the U.N. Security Council. Like the IMF, it makes momentous decisions that have global impact. Any decision the Security Council takes under Chapter VII of the U.N. Charter is mandatory on all countries of the world. The Security Council's political and security responsibilities match the IMF's financial role. When the Security Council intervenes effectively in conflicts, it saves lives, as it did in East Timor and Sierra Leone. When it does not, it can contribute to disaster, as in the case of the genocide in Rwanda.

The time has come for America to honestly evaluate whether it has used its enormous power in the Security Council to promote global interests (as the institutional responsibility of the Security Council dictates) or the narrow national interests of America. It was an archaic misjudgment to believe that turbulence in a faraway country could not affect a first world metropolis. Afghanistan in the 1990s was treated as a strategic orphan. Osama bin Laden was given a free hand to move around. Now, Afghanistan may have been fixed temporarily. But there are other "failed states" in the making. In the past, the U.N. Security Council would intervene selectively, only when the direct interests of the major powers were affected. In a shrinking globe, the Security Council must develop a more consistent set of principles on when and how to intervene. American leadership to achieve such consistency is vital. The financial resources required would be meager. By not intervening in Afghanistan over the course of the 1990s, the United Nations may have saved a few hundred million dollars. On the other side of the ledger, does anyone know yet the real economic costs of 9/11? Was it a hundred billion dollars? Or was it a trillion dollars?

A more consistent record of conflict prevention and resolution will cost the world little, but the global benefits of being perceived to be minding the interests of the entire global village would be immensely helpful in rebuilding America's prestige and moral standing.

In conceiving the Bretton Woods institutions and the United Nations, America did more than create a few critical global institutions. It also established a code of conduct that over the past half century or more has made the world a more civilized place. War has not been abolished. It may never go away as a feature of the barren landscape. But wars have become distinctively less frequent since the American-inspired U.N. Charter was drafted ". . . to save succeeding generations from the scourge of war, which twice in our lifetime has brought untold sorrow to mankind . . . ." Today, it is almost inconceivable that any two modern developed societies would go to war against each other.

I come from Southeast Asia, which has sometimes been described as the Balkans of Asia. In fact, it is much more diverse than the Balkans of Europe. Every major religion is represented in Southeast Asia: Hindu, Muslim, Christian, Buddhist, Confucian. Yet, since the Association of Southeast Asian Nations (ASEAN) was created in 1967, no two ASEAN nations have gone to war against each other. This is an enormous achievement. There are many reasons for it: leadership, luck, the strong American presence in Southeast Asia. No single factor on its own explains the lack of war. But it is undoubtedly clear that the decision of the ASEAN countries to adopt the code of conduct that America had offered to the world after World War II made a huge difference.

When the European states were powerful, they conquered the world. When America was powerful, it did not. America was probably the first power in history to demonstrate that it could achieve satisfactory dominance without having to invade and colonize. At the end of World War II, American international lawyers wove into both the U.N. Charter and prevailing international law the key principles that would guide the use of force in international relations.

The delegitimization of the arbitrary use of force was one of America's greatest contributions to the world.

That is one reason why the Iraq war had such a shattering impact on America's standing in the world. When America decided to go to war despite having failed to get an enabling U.N. resolution, America tore a hole in the very consensus that had been an American gift to the world. It is almost impossible to assess the costs. Maybe it will not alter the course of human history. The progressive delegitimization of the arbitrary use of force that the world has grown accustomed to may well continue apace. But it is also conceivable that America may have created a loophole that other nations may also use when it serves their short-term interest to do so. Robert Bolt, in his famous play *A Man for All Seasons*, portrays a remarkable dialogue between Sir Thomas More and his nephew, Roper:

ROPER: So now you'd give the Devil benefit of law.
MORE: Yes. What would you do? Cut a great road through the law to get after the Devil?
ROPER: I'd cut down every law in England to do that.
MORE: Oh? And when the last law was down—and the Devil turned round on you—where would you hide, Roper, the laws all being flat? This country's planted thick with laws from coast to coast—Man's laws, not God's—and if you cut them down—and you're just the man to do it—d'you really think you could stand upright in the winds that would blow then? Yes, I'd give the Devil benefit of law, for my own safety's sake.

To regain the goodwill of the world, America must nurture and strengthen its commitment to act by the code that it designed for the world. Given the enormous stake that America has in a stable and civilized world order, America should once again be in the forefront, as it was at the end of World War II, in promoting greater respect for international law. International law imposes significant constraints on the unilateral use of power. But by demonstrating adherence to the constraints imposed by international law, the sole superpower also encourages every other nation to accept them. Americans are acutely familiar with the rule of law in their own communities. They know that the rule of law works only when it is applied equally to every citizen, rich and poor, weak and powerful. Having created a web of international law, it ultimately will serve American interests and global interests to observe and strengthen it. American leadership in this area again can win for America significant global goodwill.

The fourth strategic decision that America has to make may well be the easiest: to continue building the best human society ever seen in history. American society is not perfect. It is a human society. It has many flaws. But many people believe that the human society that comes closest to perfection is America. To me, the virtue that most deserves to be celebrated is the belief of each American citizen that he has equal worth to any other American citizen, regardless of birth, wealth, or circumstance. The self-confidence of the American individual citizen is a joy to behold. You see it everywhere.

I've lived for over ten years in New York. In other parts of the world, the men who open the doors for you come from the lower classes. Their eyes look down in a sort of implicit bow as they open the doors for the richer, more valued, occupants of the building. New York doormen never look down. They look you straight in the eye and behave as total equals. They are happy to trade stories, either about the latest sports events, their recent vacation in the Caribbean, or the college successes of their children. They may work for other Americans in the building, indeed receive tips from fellow Americans, but they possess not an iota of inferiority.

This is an enormous leap upwards in the human evolutionary ladder. For most of the history of humankind, virtually every human society has created strong class divisions. America has largely escaped the pernicious effects of class stratification. American society is constantly churning. In any other society, the Rockefellers and the Vanderbilts would feel that they have an eternal place on the top of the social and economic ladder. Today, they have to give way to the Bill Gateses and Warren Buffets of America. America always celebrates new success stories. Larry Page and Sergey Brin of Google could soon replace Bill Gates and Warren Buffet. This is the main reason why virtually every ambitious young man or woman who is disadvantaged by his domestic social framework wants to come to America. For most human societies today, one's destiny is determined at birth. There is room for mobility but it is limited.

The world would be a much darker place if it were deprived of the American dream. All human societies are, in one form or another, prisoners of their past. The ability of any human society to progress forward depends on its ability to escape from the dead hand of the past. Asian societies are blessed with long and rich histories. But these long histories also act as a brake on embracing the future. Many Asians had to leave their own societies and live in America to begin to realize their own potential.

America is therefore an atypical human society, unlike any other. Until recently, it has served as a powerful beacon, pointing to a future for all of humankind. That is its essence, its real mission: to remain true to its soul and remain an extraordinary society. Over time, all of humankind will emulate the best features of American society. All that America has to do for the next hundred years is to keep the flame alight. If it does this, it will receive humankind's resounding applause and thanks at the end of the twenty-first century.

FIGURE 1. Population size and age distribution for 1950, 2000, and 2050 in an anticipated enlarged European Union of 25 countries and in 25 countries in North Africa and West Asia.

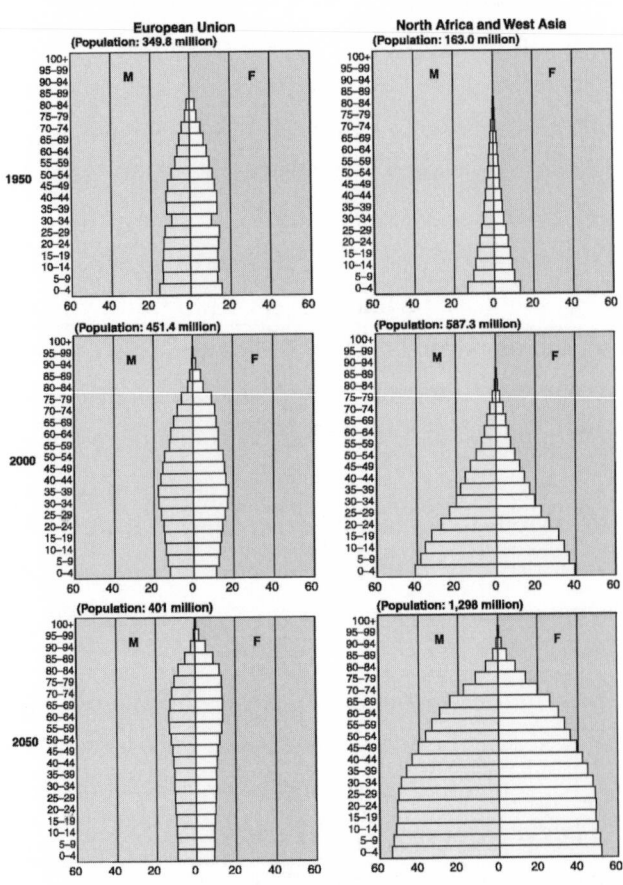

This chart, taken from Joel Cohen's article, illustrates vividly the long-term consequences of differing birth rates in Europe and North Africa/West Asia. It can also help to explain Europe's obsession with the Islamic world.

Notes

INTRODUCTION

1. Thomas L. Friedman, "A Theory of Everything," *New York Times*, June 1, 2003.

HOW AMERICA BENEFITS THE WORLD

1. Anneliese Rohrer, "A Boy from Graz," *New York Times*, October 9, 2003, p. A37.
2. John Leland, "Why America Sees the 'Silver Lining,'" *New York Times*, June 13, 2000, Week in Review, p. 1.
3. Vartan Gregorian, *The Road to Home: My Life and Times* (New York: Simon & Schuster, 2003).
4. Elie Krakowski, "Pro-American Sentiments Coming Out of Closet in Iran," *Fair Comment*, February 3, 2004.

HOW AMERICA HAS HARMED THE WORLD

1. Henry Kissinger, *Diplomacy* (New York: Touchstone Books, Simon & Schuster, 1995), p. 804.
2. Ibid., p. 805.
3. Norm Dixon, "How the CIA Created Osama bin Laden," Green Left

Weekly (Online edition: http://www.greenleft.org.au/back/2001/465/465p15. htm.

4. Cited in Peter L. Bergen, *Holy War Inc: Inside the Secret World of Osama bin Laden* (New York: Simon & Schuster, 2001).

5. Ahmed Rashid, *New York Review of Books*, 51, no. 9, May 27, 2004, p. 19, review of Steve Coll, *Ghost Wars: The Secret History of the CIA, Afghanistan, and Bin Laden, from the Soviet Invasion to September 10, 2001* (New York: Penguin Books, 2004).

6. Ziauddin Sardar and Merryl Wyn Davies, *Why Do People Hate America?* (Cambridge, England: Icon Books, 2002), p. 7.

7. Rick Rowden, "Kicking the IMF and World Bank Where It Hurts," *Economic Justice News Online*, April 2003.

8. Fareed Zakaria, *The Future of Freedom* (New York: W. W. Norton & Co., 2003), p. 118.

9. Ziauddin Sardar and Merryl Wyn Davies, op. cit., n. 6, pp. 9–10.

AMERICA AND ISLAM

1. Chris Patten, "Islam and the West—At the Crossroads." Lecture in Oxford on May 24, 2004.

2. Speech delivered by Daniel Rose, chairman, Rose Associates Inc., on November 21, 2003, at Philanthropy Day 2003, sponsored by the Association of Fundraising Professionals in Uniondale, New York.

3. Quoted in "Lost in Translation: The Two Minds of Bernard Lewis" by Ian Buruma, *New Yorker*, June 14 and 21, 2004, p. 184.

4. Husain Haqqani, "Islam's Medieval Outposts," *Foreign Policy*, November/December 2002, pp. 58–64.

5. Amadou Toumani Toure and Blaise Compaore, "Your Farm Subsidies Are Strangling Us," *New York Times*, July 11, 2003, A17.

6. "Talking Turkey," *Financial Times*, May 18, 2004, p. 12.

7. Deborah Sontag, "The Erdogan Experiment," *New York Times Magazine*, May 11, 2003, p. 42.

8. Cited in *The 9/11 Commission Report—Final Report of the National Commission on Terrorist Attacks Upon the United States*, Chapter 12: "What to Do? A Global Strategy," July 2004, p. 377 (http://www. washintonpost.com/wp-srv/nation/911report/documents/911Report_ Ch12.pdf).

9. Richard Bernstein, "Tape, Probably bin Laden's, Offers 'Truce' to Europe," *New York Times*, April 16, 2004, p. 3.

10. Susan Sachs, "Poll Finds Hostility Hardening Towards U.S. Policies," *New York Times*, March 17, 2004, p. 3.

11. The Middle East Media Research Institute (MEMRI) Special Dispatch Series, No. 767, August 20, 2004.

12. *The 9/11 Commission Report—Final Report of the National Commission on Terrorist Attacks Upon the United States*, Chapter 12: "What to Do? A Global Strategy," op. cit., no. 8, pp. 374–375.

13. Ibid., pp. 363–364.

14. *Cairo Times* (Egypt), quoted in MEMRI Special Dispatch, No. 647, January 21, 2004.

15. Eden Naby and Richard N. Frye, "The Martyr Complex," *New York Times*, September 14, 2003, p. 11.

AMERICA AND CHINA

1. Thomas L. Friedman, "Pray that China's Bubble Won't Burst," *International Herald Tribune*, May 3, 2004, p. 8.

2. Thomas L. Friedman, "Maids vs. Occupiers," *New York Times*, June 17, 2004, p. A29.

THE NATURE OF AMERICAN POWER

1. Gerard Baker, "Where did all the love for America go?" *Financial Times*, September 11, 2003, p. 21.

2. "The American Prison Camp," *New York Times*, October 16, 2003, p. A28.

3. *Financial Times*, May 1/2, 2004, p. 1.

4. Reed Brody, "Prisoner Abuse: What about the other secret U.S. prisons?" *International Herald Tribune*, May 4, 2004, p. 8.

5. William J. Broad, "Ideas and Trends: Chain Reaction," *New York Times*, August 3, 2003, pg. 1.

6. Juan Forero, "Latin America Graft and Poverty Trying Patience with Democracy," *New York Times*, June 24, 2004, p. A1.

7. William Pfaff, "Africa Needs Europe to Get Involved Again in a Different Spirit," *International Herald Tribune*, August 15, 1994, p. 4.

8. Robert E. Rubin and Jacob Weisberg, *In an Uncertain World* (New York: Random House, 2003), p. 248.

9. Joseph E. Stiglitz, *Globalization and Its Discontents* (New York: W. W. Norton & Company, 2002), p. 90.

10. Ibid., p. 128.

11. Peter Waldman, "Power and Peril: America's Supremacy and Its Limits," *Wall Street Journal*, February 11, 2004, p. A1.

12. Susan Sachs, "Poll Finds Hostility Hardening Towards U.S. Policies," *New York Times*, March 17, 2004, p. 3.

13. Pew Research Center for the People and the Press, "A Year after Iraq War: Mistrust of America in Europe Ever Higher, Muslim Anger Persists," Washington, D.C., March 16, 2004, p. 2.

14. Joel E. Cohen, "Human Population: The Next Half Century," *Science*, November 14, 2003, vol. 302, p. 172.

MANAGING AMERICAN POWER

1. Kofi Annan, *Millennium Report of the Secretary-General of the U.N. 'We the Peoples': The Role of the United Nations in the 21st Century*, Section II, Globalisation and Governance, pp. 14–15.

2. David Leonhardt, "Globalization Hits a Political Speed Bump," *New York Times,* June 1, 2003, p. 1.

3. "The Case Against King Cotton," *New York Times*, December 7, 2003, p. 12.

4. Elizabeth Becker, "Western Farmers Fear Third World Challenges to Subsidies," *New York Times*, September 9, 2003, p. A8.

5. *New York Times*, September 9, 2003.

6. Fareed Zakaria, *New York Times Book Review*, April 11, 2004, p. 8, review of Hans Blix, *Disarming Iraq* (New York: Pantheon Books, 2004).

7. Thomas L. Friedman, "Israel's New Road Map: Take the High Ground," *The Indian Express,* June 14, 2004.

THE WAY AHEAD

1. Anne-Marie Slaughter, *A New World Order* (Princeton: Princeton University Press, 2004), p. 4.

2. Julian Hewitt, "Ubuntu of Globalisation—When a Superpower Sneezes We Shudder," *International Herald Tribune,* July 31/August 1, 2004, p. 4.

3. Edward Wong, "The Reach of War: Rebellion," *New York Times,* June 28, 2004, p. A9.

4. Robert Wright, "Two Years Later, A Thousand Years Ago," *New York Times,* September 11, 2003, p. A25.

Index

Index

IMF and, 206
political and economic, 105, 106,
147–148
social and political, 145, 165
See also Destabilization; Instability
Statue of Liberty, 179
Steinberg, Jim, 155
Stiglitz, Joseph, 41, 153, 155
Stinger missiles, 36
Subjugation, liberation *v.*, 10–11
Subsidies, 204
cotton, 76–77, 168–171, 197
Success
hope and motivation as ingredients
for, 18
meritocracy and, 1–5, 7–8, 19–21
stories, American, 211
survey on, 4
Sudanese pharmaceutical factory,
bombing of, 136
Suez crisis of 1956, 62
Suharto, President, 40, 43–45, 154–155,
157
Suicide bombings, 64, 92
Summers, Lawrence, 42, 154
Swan, Christopher, 205
Swift, Dean, 24
Syplisg, Charles, 205–206
Syria, 11
torture in, 133

Taba Accords, 48
Tahir, Mohamed, 75
Taiwan, 101, 107–111, 123
Taleban, 37–38, 85, 92, 149
the Northern Alliance and, 72
Omar as leader of, 75
Al-Qaeda and, 86
Tang Dynasty, 100, 159
Taylor, Charles, 149
Technology
American, 36, 38, 87, 97, 126, 140, 167
American power and, 140

Japanese, 139
military, 36
nuclear, 29
Western, Islam and, 69
Telhami, Shibley, 188–189
Terrorism, 193
in Asia, 151–152
battle against, 85–86
bin Laden and, 57, 98
CIA and, 37
fears of, 179
increased, 190
Islam and, 33, 80–81, 85–86, 188
training camps for, 34
Textile manufacturers, 196
Thailand
America's relationship with, 182
financial crisis, 40–43, 45–46, 206
A Theory of Justice (Rawls), 6–7
Third World
democracy in, 177
influence in, 43
political collapse/misrule in, 148,
150
poverty in, 20, 169–170
rich in, 6
"the Third rail," of politics, 176, 177
Thumbo, Erikanger, 169
Tiananmen tragedy, 118, 132–133
Tibet, 107, 108
Tolbert, William R., Jr., 148
Torture
definitions of, 132
of Al-Qaeda suspects, 133
Trade
in Asia, 12–13
global/world, 140–141, 206
Treaties
U.N. resolutions and, 140
of Westphalia, 182–183
Truman, Harry, 11, 22
Trust, rebuilding, 33
Tubman, William V.S., 148

PUBLICAFFAIRS is a publishing house founded in 1997. It is a tribute to the standards, values, and flair of three persons who have served as mentors to countless reporters, writers, editors, and book people of all kinds, including me.

I. F. STONE, proprietor of *I. F. Stone's Weekly*, combined a commitment to the First Amendment with entrepreneurial zeal and reporting skill and became one of the great independent journalists in American history. At the age of eighty, Izzy published *The Trial of Socrates*, which was a national bestseller. He wrote the book after he taught himself ancient Greek.

BENJAMIN C. BRADLEE was for nearly thirty years the charismatic editorial leader of *The Washington Post*. It was Ben who gave the *Post* the range and courage to pursue such historic issues as Watergate. He supported his reporters with a tenacity that made them fearless, and it is no accident that so many became authors of influential, best-selling books.

ROBERT L. BERNSTEIN, the chief executive of Random House for more than a quarter century, guided one of the nation's premier publishing houses. Bob was personally responsible for many books of political dissent and argument that challenged tyranny around the globe. He is also the founder and was the longtime chair of Human Rights Watch, one of the most respected human rights organizations in the world.

·   ·   ·

For fifty years, the banner of Public Affairs Press was carried by its owner, Morris B. Schnapper, who published Gandhi, Nasser, Toynbee, Truman, and about 1,500 other authors. In 1983 Schnapper was described by *The Washington Post* as "a redoubtable gadfly." His legacy will endure in the books to come.

Peter Osnos, *Publisher*